Paved with Good Intentions

PAVED WITH GOOD INTENTIONS

The NGO Experience in North Korea

Edited by
L. Gordon Flake and Scott Snyder

Published under the auspices of the Mansfield Center for Pacific Affairs

PRAEGER

C. Mahaffey
J. Sterrett
23 May 04

Westport, Connecticut
London

Library of Congress Cataloging-in-Publication Data

Paved with good intentions : the NGO experience in North Korea / edited by L. Gordon
  Flake and Scott Snyder.
      p. cm.
    "Published under the auspices of the Mansfield Center for Pacific Affairs."
    Includes bibliographical references and index.
    ISBN 0–275–98157–6
    1. Humanitarian assistance—Korea (North) 2. Non-governmental organizations—Korea
  (North) I. Flake, L. Gordon, 1967– . II. Snyder, Scott, 1964– .
HV415.6.P38 2003
361.7'7'095193—dc21   2003053626

British Library Cataloguing in Publication Data is available.

Library of Congress Catalog Card Number: 2003053626
ISBN: 0–275–98157–6

First published in 2003

Praeger Publishers, 88 Post Road West, Westport, CT 06881
An imprint of Greenwood Publishing Group, Inc.
www.praeger.com

Printed in the United States of America

The paper used in this book complies with the
Permanent Paper Standard issued by the National
Information Standards Organization (Z39.48–1984).

10 9 8 7 6 5 4 3 2 1

Contents

Preface

With news headlines dominated by reports of the latest developments in what appears to be a new nuclear crisis on the Korean peninsula, it is difficult to recall a time that may ultimately be regarded as a temporary lull in tensions there. The conclusion of a "Framework Agreement" between the United States and the Democratic People's Republic of Korea (DPRK) in October of 1994 helped defuse the immediate tensions surrounding the previous nuclear crisis and also served as a foundation for an unprecedented expansion in ties, not only between the United States and North Korea, but also between North Korea and the international community. The strongest evidence for this came when, in response to chronic food shortages and severe flooding in the summer of 1995, North Korea appealed to the international community for help. In addition to the response of national governments and international organizations such as the United Nations' World Food Program, an unprecedented number of nongovernmental organizations (NGOs) joined the effort to address North Korea's humanitarian needs.

As the number of NGOs working in North Korea expanded, it became increasingly apparent that their interaction with the DPRK government and the scope of their activities within the country offered an unprecedented window upon what is perhaps the most isolated regime on earth. While smaller in scale than the activities of the major international humanitarian and development agencies, the rapid engagement of the NGO community in a variety of activities ranging from agriculture to energy to medicine promised not only a relatively broad view of a wide geographic swath of North Korea but also insights into different sectors of society.

This edited volume is the product of a two-year study on the activities of NGOs working in and with the DPRK. Based on the presumption that the unprecedented opening of North Korea to such NGOs would lead to a greater understanding of the situation and possible changes occurring in North Korea, the authors of this work first conducted a broad survey of the available literature from U.S., European, and

South Korean NGOs. We then held extensive interviews with individual NGO representatives who had spent time in North Korea and organized a series of workshops that convened NGO representatives for sector-specific discussions on the situation in North Korea. Without intending to exaggerate the role of NGOs, this study intentionally focused primarily on the role of NGO activities. As such, it is not intended to be a full accounting of the international response to North Korea's food crisis, nor a complete portrayal of North Korea's international relations during the period. Still, one advantage to addressing a regime as relatively isolated as North Korea is that even small amounts of information tend to have value and advance understanding.

During the process of preparing this manuscript for publication, the apparent relevance of this work has seemed to ebb and flow. In the heady days immediately following the historic inter-Korean summit between South Korean President Kim Dae Jung and North Korean leader Kim Jong Il, it appeared that the efforts of the NGO community might be quickly overshadowed by the pace of inter-Korean reconciliation. At present, many of the hopes that some NGOs seemed to harbor for a more open and engaged North Korea appear to have been dashed, or at least temporarily placed on hold during the current crisis.

The study and the publication of this book were made possible by a grant from the Smith Richardson Foundation, as well as the support of the Asia Foundation and the Maureen and Mike Mansfield Foundation. Our particular thanks go to Allan Song at the Smith Richardson Foundation for his support and his appropriate prodding as challenges arose.

As with any book, the names of the authors on the cover do not reflect the network of friends and colleagues that are truly responsible for bringing this effort to fruition. This project was conceived by my co-author, Scott Snyder, who provided the lion's share of the vision and intellectual heft through both the study and the process of preparing the final reports. It was our pleasure to work with two outstanding scholars, Dr. Chung Oknim, who reports on the activities of Korean NGOs, and Dr. Michael Schloms, who brings a continental perspective with his summary of the role of European NGOs.

Thanks also go to Professor Andrew Walder at Stanford University, who met with all the principals involved in the project and helped us frame our interview process in an academically consistent, if not entirely rigorous manner.

I would be remiss if I did not also recognize my colleagues at the Mansfield Center for Pacific Affairs. Director of Communications Mary-Jane Atwater shepherded this project though the editing and publication process. Program Associate Nia Lizanna and interns Dena Kram and Iku Fujimatsu managed the logistics of the workshops as well as the early editing and formatting of the chapters. I also extend our gratitude to our colleagues in the Asia Foundation's Seoul Office, in particular EunJung Cahill Che, Ban Seon-Eun and Moon Chun Sang.

L. Gordon Flake
The Mansfield Center for Pacific Affairs, Washington, D.C.

Chapter One
The NGO Experience in North Korea

Scott Snyder

INTRODUCTION

The Democratic People's Republic of Korea (DPRK), or North Korea, is widely perceived as a virtually inaccessible, hermetically sealed nation with a monolithic structure of political control. The leadership is so determined to maintain power that it has constructed an incredibly long-running cult of personality and an elaborate system of leader worship that does not allow political space for challengers and barely tolerates private pursuits divorced from the life of the state. The primary message of the state, through a system of political education that pervades every aspect of existence in North Korea, is that life is not worth living without devotion to the "Dear Leader," Kim Jong Il. The severe personal consequences of failure to recognize and adhere to this central tenet of life reinforce the message in stark terms. Fealty to the leader and the state are prerequisites for favored positions within the state structure. Class background and family connections have a determining influence on where one lives and what one does for a living, and determine one's standard of living, wages, and rations. In a resource-poor system where the pie has contracted over the course of the past decade, the only way for most to ensure individual survival is to move closer to the center.

The North Korean political philosophy, authored and propagated by North Korea's founding leader, Kim Il Sung, is known as *juche*. It was formulated in direct response to the profound shock that accompanied Korea's loss of sovereignty and colonization by Japan from 1910 to Korea's liberation from Japanese domination at the end of World War II. The main idea of *juche* is to elevate human beings as the central motivating force, or subject—not object—of action, but that in the process promotes the North Korean leader as the singular driving force for independent action on which everyone else is dependent.[1] To most observers, the DPRK appears isolated and trapped in its own world, unready and unwilling to participate in the global community or to allow any visitors except those bearing gifts in honor of the Great and Dear Leaders. This widely held external perception of the DPRK is reflected in *The Economist*'s June 2000 cover story on the inter-Korean summit and Kim Jong Il's emergence on the public stage, entitled "Greetings, Earthlings."[2]

In its isolation, North Korea's "Kim dynasty" is the natural successor to the "Hermit Kingdom," the name given to Korea by westerners who tried to open the Chosun dynasty to international commerce in the late 19th century. Yet the isolation sought by Chosun dynasty leaders, who tried to protect their traditions from foreign encroachment, ultimately could not be maintained in the face of the gradual penetration by the major powers, led by Japan. The eventual result was the dissolution of Chosun dynasty Korea. Will North Korea's current leadership fare better in its quest for survival and autonomy? With the collapse of communism and the end of the Cold War, North Korea's isolation was exacerbated and its leaders were left with the unenviable job of shepherding a failed ideology and system, bereft of the socialist goodwill of its closest neighbors, which had been the foundation for the country's relative economic stability through the 1980s. Without transfer payments or barter trade with the socialist bloc and with increasing pressure to conduct economic relations according to market principles, North Korea's gross domestic product (GDP) began a precipitous, decade-long slide to barely half its previous size between 1989 and 1998, tightening the noose of dependence on the state system as the only means for economic survival in the absence of any alternative.

Natural disasters, including torrential typhoon rains in August 1995, provided the pretext for North Korea's opening to food assistance from the international community, which began to respond to North Korean pleas in early 1996. This opening to international humanitarian assistance was an unprecedented public admission of the Pyongyang leadership's inability to meet the needs of its people.

International humanitarian workers arrived in Pyongyang ill prepared for what they found. Unlike the situation in other humanitarian emergencies, North Korea's political system remained intact, weathered the economic disaster, and imposed strict limits on the interaction of humanitarian aid workers with the North Korean people. The immediate prior experience of many humanitarian aid workers in Africa and other parts of the world did not prepare them for the cultural, political, and linguistic barriers that existed in North Korea.

The voluntary admission of international humanitarian aid workers—in combination with the involuntary flow of desperately hungry North Koreans across the border with China—marked the beginning of the end of North Korea's hermetic isolation and the dawn of a new challenge to the survival of its political system. Previously, there had been virtually no "external window" or on-the-ground foreign presence in North Korea, beyond a few diplomats in their isolated diplomatic enclave at the center of Pyongyang. Although the overriding interest of humanitarian aid workers from United Nations organizations and nongovern-mental organizations (NGOs) was to help North Koreans who were facing starvation and to forestall an even greater humanitarian disaster, their entry into the country constituted an unprecedented opportunity for outsiders to directly experience the situation there. Foreign representatives of humanitarian aid organizations responding to the crisis gained a rare foothold in North Korea, but even that access has been grudgingly permitted, gradual, and, in some cases, reversible. Despite the good intentions with which aid workers came to North Korea and despite the North Korean government's decision to allow them in, the presence of humanitarian aid workers was perceived as a threat to an embattled regime that had long regarded direct contact with the outside as a mortal danger to its ability to maintain political control and loyalty among the people. Humanitarian aid constituted a direct threat to the myth of *juche* upon which the North Korean ideology was built and threatened to undermine the central role of the state. Thus, for the North Korean leadership, humanitarian assistance and the physical presence of outsiders in Pyongyang and elsewhere were intensely political.

Likewise, the opportunity to enter North Korea, even for humanitarian reasons, was understandably viewed by the United States and South Korea through a political lens, despite the pretensions and aspirations associated with the Reagan-era dictum, "a hungry child knows no politics." NGO donors also came to North Korea with a wide range of perspectives and preconceptions, shaped by the politics of humanitarian assistance and their experiences in other parts of the world, experiences that in many cases were not directly transferable to the political environment in North Korea. It soon became clear that, regardless of motivation, all sides would eventually view aid through the lens of politics, and even those who came to North Korea without political motives would ultimately acknowledge that the nature and concerns of the North Korean political system inevitably created dilemmas in managing programs inside the DPRK. Although the Reagan-era dictum was intended to make space for humanitarian concerns apart from the sphere of politics, the North Korean regime's ringing and consistent rejection of that premise ultimately has made it impossible to separate humanitarian assistance from political considerations.

Thus, despite the urgency of the humanitarian disaster, the major initial challenge faced in North Korea was to find ways to create space for a humanitarian effort that would allow the needs of suffering people to be placed above politics. This was the most difficult, and perhaps unexpected, concession that the North Korean leadership faced as a result of its decision to appeal for humanitarian assistance. It spawned a battle over monitoring and distribution that still rages and is at the heart of the ongoing debate over how and whether humanitarian aid can be separated from the political objectives of the North Korean regime. Regardless of whether the motives of the humanitarian aid community in North Korea were purely altruistic or tinged by political concerns, the primary North Korean objectives in dealing with UN organization representatives and NGO monitors in the country were clear: minimize contact and channels of communication with ordinary people and control access to the broader North Korean public, while drawing in as many resources as possible.

OBJECTIVES AND OUTLINE OF THIS STUDY

This research project attempts to independently examine the impact of NGO and UN humanitarian relief efforts in North Korea and to draw lessons from those experiences that might increase understanding of North Korea's structure and system for managing NGO activities. Another objective is to draw together and catalog information about the various NGOs that are working in North Korea. We hope these lessons and this information will be useful in future inter-actions with North Korea.

Past research efforts have examined NGO experiences from particular national or issue-oriented perspectives; this effort aims to be comprehensive in its treatment and comparison of experiences, to provide a more complete understanding of the types of work that are ongoing and how North Korea responds to representatives from different countries, regions, and ethnicities. On the basis of interviews with NGO and UN representatives and independent research focused on the U.S., European, and South Korean experiences, each of the chapter authors describes the context, experience, and activities of the respective NGO communities in dealing with North Korea and analyzes and explains the peculiarities, processes, and results of this interaction. The chapters identify the obstacles faced by humani-tarian relief workers and explore the impact of NGO efforts on North Korea, including whether there is evidence of change in North Korean policies as a result of UN and NGO efforts. Through a better understanding of North Korean efforts to direct, channel, and control humanitarian interests and activities, we hope to construct a more detailed picture of its internal political structure for dealing with the outside world and its capacity for managing recovery from a total breakdown of its economic system. North Korea's interaction with the international humani-tarian assistance community—as a first step in the country's interaction with the outside world—may determine the extent, direction, and pace of expanded North Korean interaction with the international community.

The NGOs that responded to North Korea's humanitarian crisis are spread out over Europe, the United States, South Korea, China, Japan, Canada, and Australia. They have had widely varying interactions with their North Korean counterparts—composed almost exclusively of North Korean government officials with the special task of managing international NGO representatives—based on their inter-ests and expertise, but North Korea has responded to many of these organizations with similar tactics and objectives. A primary conclusion that may be drawn from this comparative study is that working directly with the North Korean regime and its system of political control is a polarizing and troubling experience for most people who have prolonged interaction with the North Korean bureaucracy. Regardless of whether an organization's motive for entering North Korea was primarily humanitarian or political, the practical response to interacting with the North Korean regime and the political control system set into place to manage NGO actors has been either to walk away and condemn North Korea's failed system as a morally bankrupt manifestation of cruelty, depravity, and exploitation of its own people, or to hold one's nose and seek cooperation in forms that may ultimately create more economic capacity and political and humanitarian space for the average North Korean. This combination of public condemnation and continued cooperation to help pry open the regime by giving material assistance in ways that may benefit the North Korean people is precisely the mix of incentives and criticisms that is likely to pose the greatest ongoing threat to the regime's survival. Unfortunately, the institutionalized relationships of international organizations with the central government sometimes result in a third type of response: the provision of material support for reasons of political expediency or narrow self-interest in ways that directly reinforce the North Korean leadership and are designed to prop up or sustain the regime.

EVOLUTION OF NGO INVOLVEMENT IN NORTH KOREA

The NGO presence in North Korea was catalyzed primarily by the DPRK request to the international community for assistance following the 1995 floods. Because there had been virtually no prior NGO presence in North Korea, most NGOs began their operations in cooperation with or through the UN World Food Program (WFP), which itself was only beginning to establish its operations in North Korea, although the UN had been represented for many years through a small office of the UN Development Program (UNDP) and through a few minor programs carried out by other UN agencies.

The first and most critical phase of North Korea's food crisis occurred during 1996 and 1997; at this time, many NGOs made their initial entry, assessed needs and determined possible responses, and regularized their procedures, areas of coverage, and operations. This critical phase of NGO operations was characterized by the negotiation of entry arrangements into the country, a complex process that generally was managed during the initial phases via cooperation with the WFP, an agency with vast resources and experience in responding to African famine but little, if any, direct prior experience in Northeast Asia or Korea.

A small WFP office opened in 1996, with the initial task of setting up a distribution network and assessment process that would be able to manage the flow of humanitarian assistance into North Korea and its distribution to those most in need. Armed with a satellite phone and charged with establishing a new office that could manage oversight of food distribution throughout the DPRK, WFP representative Trevor Page and other NGO representatives were assigned to work with the newly established Flood Damage Rehabilitation Committee (FDRC), a bureaucratic entity drawn from various North Korean ministries and established by the government to manage interactions with the international humanitarian aid community. The FDRC oversaw virtually all international humanitarian relief efforts inside the country. Despite the establishment of this bureaucratic organ in the context of the outbreak of famine across the DPRK, authorities in Pyongyang followed the same procedures for managing interaction with the WFP that traditionally had been in place to control interaction between foreigners and ordinary North Korean people.

Despite emergency conditions, the FDRC required a week's notice to prepare for site visits outside of Pyongyang and insisted that only non-Korean-speaking staff be assigned to North Korea, among other requirements that did not conform to international standards for monitoring food deliveries. Professional humanitarian aid workers lodged continuous complaints; however, the FDRC steadfastly followed strict procedures for setting up visits to monitor food deliveries and managed every aspect of visitors' schedules once they arrived in the country. From the very beginning, the DPRK authorities resisted random site visits or uncontrolled interaction with aid recipients and ordinary North Korean villagers, a policy that aid workers found unacceptable but have not been able to reverse.

These procedures were applied to both international and nongovernmental organizations from the United States and Europe as they began to arrive and scout out possibilities for mounting their own response to the crisis. Because of the urgency of the crisis and their unfamiliarity with the environment in which they were working, most NGOs accepted these restrictions, while constantly pushing for greater access. In fact, because of their language deficiencies, NGO and UN aid workers in Pyongyang were necessarily dependent on cooperation with the FDRC to fulfill their mission and to manage logistics connected with food deliveries. The interaction between the FDRC and international humanitarian aid organizations thus was adversarial from its inception, since the primary task of the FDRC was to watch the international food monitors and only secondarily to help them ensure that assistance was delivered to end users. The fact that the FDRC faced overwhelming infrastructure and logistics needs and that international food monitors without knowledge of the Korean language had to rely on their FDRC colleagues in order to fill those needs made the relationships even more complicated and increased the potential for mutual mistrust.

Many NGOs sought to initiate humanitarian operations and set up permanent offices in country despite initial resistance by North Korea. Given the difficulties of setting up a resident presence in Pyongyang in the initial stages of the crisis, NGOs gathered together to negotiate with the WFP a nongovernmental monitoring office that would work under the auspices of the WFP presence in Pyongyang, eventually entitled the Food Aid Liaison Unit (FALU). This unit was established in 1997 under the supervision of a Canadian couple, Erich and Marilyn Weingartner. The FALU became the primary vehicle through which nonresident NGOs could have their aid deliveries monitored by on-the-ground staff that also worked closely with the WFP. The creation of the FALU—a hybrid unit that was nongovernmental but established under the auspices of the WFP expressly to work with NGOs—was an adaptation to the strict working environment in North Korea that provided a proxy monitoring capacity. The existence of the FALU demonstrates how certain NGOs were forced to adapt to North Korean conditions as a compromise in order to provide assistance inside the country.

During 1997 and 1998, there was a second phase of operations during which the presence of the WFP was stabilized and many NGO operations were regularized to include an in-country presence. During this period of institutionalization, most NGOs focused on regularizing their operations in North Korea and establishing permanent residency—a requirement for European NGOs that hoped to receive assistance from the European Commission's Humanitarian Aid Office (ECHO). Some NGOs eventually decided to withdraw, as was the case with the U.S. Private Voluntary Organization Consortium (PVOC), Médecins Du Monde (MDM), Médecins Sans Frontières (MSF), Action Contre La Faim (ACF), and Oxfam. This was also a period of rapid programmatic and geographical expansion of the WFP operation through Food for Work (FFW) programs. The WFP and the NGOs remained dissatisfied with the strict, minimally compliant conditions for monitoring food assistance. Moreover, the North Korean authorities kept almost a quarter of North Korean counties off limits, making no provision for international food assistance monitoring; therefore, there were no deliveries or relief to those areas. Several of the off-limits counties were connected with North Korea's military establishment or were regarded by the government as sensitive for unexplained reasons. Even at the height of the food relief effort, the WFP and other NGOs never made it to these counties, many of which may have been considered the most at risk because of their geographic inaccessibility and relative lack of supply lines.

Since the crisis, the DPRK has come to rely on food assistance contributions via the WFP to meet the structural deficit in its food production capacity, institutionalizing emergency humanitarian assistance as a component of the annual "budget" necessary to stabilize the country and feed its people. Meanwhile, the government has continued to follow the same failed economic policies and has made no major changes to its agricultural structure or policies. The most significant reform induced by international humanitarian assistance has been the introduction of double-cropping of winter barley on land that is then used for the annual rice crop. Appendix E shows that North Korea's production capacity has decreased since the floods of August 1995 and that, in the absence of significant policy or system reforms, the decline in productive capacity appears to be permanent. Appendix F shows the structural shortfall that has been identified through the WFP's annual estimates of production versus consumption needs in the DPRK. Appendix G shows how the WFP's contribution to meeting that structural deficit has been incorporated as a necessary component of North Korea's strategy for meeting its food needs. Of course, Appendix G does not record the ongoing assistance provided by the People's Republic of China (PRC) as part of its special relationship with the DPRK, which has been estimated at almost a million tons of grain annually. If one takes Chinese assistance into consideration, it is easy to see how Pyongyang appeared to outside observers to have stabilized its food supply situation beginning in 1998–99, the year in which WFP contributions alone came close to closing North Korea's estimated cereal deficit. Despite North Korea's apparent stabilization, based on observations of aid workers in

Pyongyang, it is clear from these figures that without agricultural and economic reforms that encourage increased production inside North Korea or increased international trade to meet its cereal deficit, the UN WFP has now become an essential crutch upon which North Korea depends for its survival, while facing diminished structural pressure to engage in system reforms.

The stabilization of North Korea at a level that still required international humanitarian assistance to help the country meet its needs posed a dilemma that prevented some NGOs from being able to justify a continued presence in the DPRK. Complicating NGO decisions during this period was the fact that little had changed in the formal procedures by which the FDRC "handled" outside monitors since humanitarian assistance had begun to arrive in country, although certain representatives reported occasional lapses in enforcement of these rules (such as Korean-speakers being allowed in) as the processes and relationships between specific monitors and their FDRC handlers became more routinized. The frustrations of the NGO community with the limits on their access and efforts to conduct monitoring activities came to a head in November 1998, when the NGOs issued a combined statement of humanitarian principles in the DPRK. This statement was precipitated by the highly public decision of MSF to withdraw from the DPRK on the grounds that conditions and access were unsuitable to allow MSF to freely conduct its humanitarian work. As the food situation inside North Korea gradually began to stabilize—despite ongoing shortages and continued willingness to receive handouts—several NGOs began to reevaluate their operations in North Korea or to draw down their assistance and end their operations.

But as the situation became more stable, the FDRC became more and more intransigent in its demands. It became clear that toleration of the NGO presence was closely tied to the amount and perceived value of aid being provided to the country. Another factor was that as more NGO representatives entered North Korea to deliver assistance, the FDRC itself was overextended by the number of NGO delegations and individuals it was responsible for monitoring. As the FDRC was stretched thin by a lack of qualified personnel to manage NGO delegations, the likelihood increased that "mistakes" would be made or that the FDRC simply could not manage the sheer volume of visitors connected with NGO efforts. Conversely, as the WFP effort became regularized and expanded, the difficulty of dealing with individual NGOs was not worth the effort. The WFP effort expanded during this period to become one of the largest operations in the world.

Ironically, North Korea's stabilization and recovery during 1998 and 1999 actually sharpened the fundamental dilemma for NGOs that had decided to participate in international food assistance operations in North Korea in ways that underscored the impossibility of separating the humanitarian effort from political considerations. Given the continued political control of the regime over the system and process for distributing humanitarian assistance to people in need, what were the intended purposes of food aid from the perspective of NGOs and the UN, and what was the actual impact of the assistance given? Were the UN and NGOs able to achieve their humanitarian purposes in North Korea apart from politics, or were they subject to manipulation by all sides, including the DPRK government and the ultimate sources of funding—governmental contributors to the WFP, including the largest donor, the U.S. government?

While use of the traditional government distribution system for delivering goods to the people may have been efficient and was certainly a luxury not found in other failed systems from the perspective of humanitarian assistance workers, it inevitably raised questions about whether international assistance was being used for political purposes to prop up a regime that might be on the verge of collapse. These questions were laid bare by a continuing flow of refugees across the northern border of North Korea to northeastern China and by persistent rumors that the Public Distribution System (PDS) had triaged portions of the country far from Pyongyang where populations might presumably be at greatest risk. Another complicating factor was that the necessity of coping mechanisms in the absence of the PDS had opened the way for barter trade, previously outlawed by strictly enforced prohibitions. Farmers' markets (*jangmadang*) had sprouted up, stocked by barter trade across the Chinese border, and had become an alternative mechanism for procuring food, which rendered the PDS increasingly irrelevant as either a control mechanism or a source of sustenance to the population.

The period following the June 2000 inter-Korean summit saw a third wave of activity: the influx of South Korean NGO projects into North Korea. Meanwhile, international NGO efforts attempted with great difficulty to prod North Korean authorities to move from a focus on humanitarian assistance to development assistance, exchanges and training, and capacity building to forestall the recurrence of crisis and introduce systemic adjustments and reforms to ensure future sustainability. During this period, the WFP also tried to encourage the North Korean government to take an interest in programs beyond humanitarian assistance that might assist in addressing structural reform. Local UN staff in Pyongyang were able to work with the DPRK to produce a coordinated action plan designed as an appeal for development assistance through the Agricultural Recovery and Environmental Protection (AREP) plan. North Korean officials came to two UN-sponsored donor conferences to stimulate outside interest in the plan, but the documents that had been prepared looked more like central planning documents produced for budget and fundraising needs than a serious blueprint for reform of North Korea's agricultural sector. As a result, there was little interest or follow-up action on the part of prospective outside donors.

Meanwhile, an apparent breakthrough in inter-Korean relations led to the establishment of direct relationships that brought South Korean NGOs into North Korea for special projects in agricultural assistance, capacity building, and technical assistance. The South Korean visitors were not handled by the FDRC, but the objective was the same. Either the Korean Asia Pacific Peace Committee (APPC) or the Committee for Overseas Compatriots hosted South Korean visitors in specialized areas, with the objective of containing their influence and interaction with specific sectors. If anything, South Korean NGOs found that they were even more constrained in their actions than other international NGOs. The APPC was even less willing to facilitate anything more than a minimal standard of monitoring and access for South Korean donors, many of whom had been considerably more generous to and aware of specific North Korean needs and cultural sensitivities than their counterparts from Europe or the United States. The level of access of South Korean visitors inside North Korea remained severely constrained, and the frustrations over failure to receive access for monitoring purposes were severe.

OUTLINE OF THE STUDY

The following three chapters aim to develop a comprehensive understanding of NGO interaction with North Korea by examining and comparing the differing experiences of U.S., European, and South Korean NGOs.

In chapter 2, L. Gordon Flake details the complex history of U.S. NGO involvement in North Korea, describing a highly politicized policy debate and circumstances in which the U.S. government used food aid as leverage to induce the North Korean government to attend the Four-Party Talks (United States, China, North Korea, and South Korea), leaving U.S. NGOs with virtually no leverage to negotiate access arrangements or the numbers of observers who would be necessary to monitor food assistance in North Korea. North Korea in turn politicized the work of the NGOs, on the basis of both its profound mistrust of NGO intentions and its failure to understand the role, function, and nature of the U.S. NGO community. Although the PVOC, a group of American NGOs that joined together to work in North Korea, was ultimately successful in lobbying the State Department to pay more attention to North Korean famine relief, the assistance came with so many political strings that the effort was unsustainable. This failure was abetted by North Korea's strong resistance to the idea of providing resident status to a U.S. NGO, given the ongoing political confrontation and the fear that a permanent U.S. office would be used to conduct espionage against North Korea, a fear compounded by public reports of conditions in North Korea that some PVOC monitors disclosed while they were in Pyongyang. Flake notes that the most successful U.S. NGOs have been associated with U.S. religious groups such as the Latter-Day Saints Ministries, Catholic and Southern Baptist-affiliated assistance organizations, and the Korean-American church community. Given the highly politicized nature of the debate over policy toward North Korea and the failed experience of the PVOC (which was forced to pull out for a variety of reasons), it seems unlikely that there will be renewed interest in NGO involvement in North Korea in the absence of progress in the political relationship.

In chapter 3, Michael Schloms analyzes the European NGO experience in North Korea, including insights from the primarily European staffs of international organizations such as the UN agencies and the International Federation of Red Cross and Red Crescent Societies (IFRC). He emphasizes the frustrations that Europeans faced owing to lack of information and cooperation necessary to undertake humanitarian action in the DPRK. In the face of these difficulties,

Schloms outlines the factors that caused certain NGOs—such as Médecins Sans Frontières, Médecins du Monde, Action Contra la Faim, and Oxfam—to withdraw rather than work under constraints that prevented them from providing direct humanitarian assistance. Other European NGOs found that there was space for them to continue their work, especially in the field of agricultural rehabilitation, although even this work often revealed the government's continuing misplaced priority on food self-sufficiency. European policy requires European NGOs to be resident in a country in order to qualify for funding from ECHO, so a wide array of resident European NGOs are trying to carry out their work and pushing their North Korean counterparts hard for space to make the transition from humanitarian to development assistance. Schloms's general prognosis for further progress is not encouraging, given the regime's resistance and its attempts to isolate outside influences from the rest of the population.

In chapter 4, Chung Oknim describes the political circumstances surrounding the activities and role of South Korean NGOs in the context of inter-Korean relations. She describes the great difficulties faced by South Korean NGOs that sought to provide humanitarian assistance to the North before the inauguration of Republic of Korea President Kim Dae Jung, at a time when the South Korean government was strongly discouraging private assistance to North Korea. With the advent of the Sunshine Policy, South Korean NGOs received much greater space, encouragement, and even government funding for their humanitarian activities with North Korea. However, the inter-Korean summit and its aftermath have dealt major challenges to South Korean NGOs in two respects. First, in the aftermath of the summit, the North Korean focus shifted to inter-Korean official relations, leaving little room for or attention to South Korean NGO activities. Second, the downturn in the South Korean public mood in the face of a lack of inter-Korean progress, compared with expectations, has left the public apathetic about the North and has detracted from interest in South Korean NGO activities there. Chung details a range of inter-Korean projects in the areas of agricultural assistance and provision of medical relief goods that have been implemented at a nongovernmental level but also reveals the frustrations that some South Korean NGOs have faced because they have not been allowed to undertake monitoring activities even to the levels established by NGOs from Europe and the UN. Chung also conveys the more optimistic, idealistic, and patient view among South Korean NGOs regarding prospects for the future in inter-Korean relations—a view generally based on the presumption that South Korean NGO activities themselves are the key to building trust and reducing tension on the Korean Peninsula.

The final chapter draws conclusions from each of the previous chapters about the situation in North Korea and suggests lessons learned from the NGO experience thus far. This author argues that the political constraints that North Korea has placed on the activities and scope of international humanitarian activities have resulted in a polarized response within the NGO community. While some NGOs and UN agencies have opted to quietly accept the constraints and meet basic needs of some needy North Koreans while continuing to challenge and seek to create space for more effective humanitarian operations from within, others have refused to accept the constraints and have opted to leave. Although changes and gradual accommodations have been achieved by NGOs on the ground as they develop closer relationships and understanding with their counterparts, considerable internal bureaucratic resistance and suspicion of outside efforts remain, which greatly hamper the effectiveness of humanitarian work inside North Korea.

North Korean efforts to constrain NGO humanitarian efforts have been designed primarily as efforts to control information, individual movement within North Korea, and the means of production, each of which is deemed critical to political control and regime survival. Despite efforts to control and limit the political impact of NGO and UN humanitarian aid efforts, the NGO presence has provided opportunities for North Korean technocrats in selected fields to learn more about the outside world and has, in the process, yielded more information through those contacts about the situation in North Korea. These influences may catalyze greater efforts to enhance productivity and efficiency inside the North Korean system. Meanwhile, North Korean efforts to maintain political control and to limit the efforts of humanitarian workers to provide aid and opportunities for the North Korean people inevitably create resentment and opposition from international humanitarian aid workers that will reduce the amount of assistance and goodwill available to North Korea from the outside world. Through their efforts at control, North Korean authorities are actually generating the forces that will inevitably lead to greater external pressures for change.

The international humanitarian response in North Korea was the first practical vehicle through which it has become possible to work inside North Korea and therefore provides an opportunity to learn more about the needs of the country and to gauge firsthand its capacity and willingness to move forward with the system changes that are necessary for rehabilitation. The experience and influence of the humanitarian aid community have extended to policy formation in the form of an increasingly expanded database for understanding North Korea's internal structure, organization, and intentions.

Former Defense Secretary William Perry, following his review of U.S. policy toward North Korea, said, "By all odds, the best source of information that I got was from the relief agencies who were over there, not just in Pyongyang, but in the villages all over North Korea. These people are doing the work of the Lord. They are out there providing food and medicine and clothing to hundreds of thousands of needy North Koreans, and they are pretty much out in the countryside where they are reasonably free of control."[3] Perry's statement implied that relief workers had been able to gain access to the Hermit Kingdom in ways others never had and would provide the world with a window on the real North Korea. His unique role as coordinator of a review of U.S. policy toward North Korea attracted a wide range of inputs, and his statement has partially inspired this effort to analyze the impact and constraints of the NGO experience in North Korea.

NOTES

1. For a more detailed explanation of *juche,* see Oh Kong-dan and Ralph Hassig, *North Korea through the Looking Glass,* Washington, D.C.; Brookings Institution, 2000, pp. 12-40.

2. *The Economist,* June 17, 2000, cover.

3. "Former Secretary of Defense William Perry Delivers Remarks at the Woodrow Wilson Center," FDCH Political Transcripts, Nov. 29, 1999 (from Lexis research service).

Chapter Two
The Experience of U.S. NGOs in North Korea

L. Gordon Flake

INTRODUCTION

It should not be surprising that the initial experiences of U.S. NGOs in North Korea were characterized by mistrust, tension, and misunderstanding, given the nature of the North Korean regime, the history of U.S.-Democratic People's Republic of Korea (DPRK) relations, and the intense politics surrounding any interaction with the North. Although the circumstances and experiences of U.S. NGOs in North Korea were unique and perhaps not widely applicable beyond the Korean Peninsula, there are many lessons from these experiences that might assist in avoiding similar misunderstandings in future interactions with the DPRK.

Most U.S. humanitarian NGOs were not prepared for the working environment they found in North Korea when the opportunity to enter first came in fall 1995 and early 1996. Humanitarian NGOs had extensive experience dealing with crisis situations in Africa, Latin America, and Southeast Asia, but isolated, socialist North Korea was an atypical aid recipient and constituted a unique environment for humanitarian work. In other regions where U.S. NGOs had worked, famine often resulted from natural disasters, failed political systems, or a combination of the two, resulting in mass migration and refugee flows that made both the need and the solution relatively straightforward. Often such crises took place in war zones or in countries in varying states of anarchy, giving a clear mission to those providing assistance and putting the impetus on logistical capacity to deliver the most effective forms of sustenance at the points of greatest need.

In contrast, throughout the worst periods of the food shortage in North Korea, the DPRK government remained in full control—at least of the foreign community in North Korea, if not its own distribution system—and it continues today to balance the need for assistance with a deep suspicion of the outside world and a heavily institutionalized inclination toward state secrecy. Although the DPRK initially opened its doors with desperate pleas for humanitarian assistance,

DPRK officials remained profoundly skeptical of outsiders and had a mandate to limit NGO access that made the relationship inherently challenging. The decision to solicit and accept assistance from outsiders constituted a fundamental challenge and overt contradiction to the regime's stated history and ideology. While there had always been a willingness to make special exceptions to the *juche*[1] ideology, which appeared to prohibit relying on handouts from other nations, the solicitation of assistance—particularly from hostile states—required DPRK officials to address deeply ingrained institutional, historical, cultural, and political barriers to access. The effect was a DPRK government that often seemed to be reaching out with an open hand, while wrapping itself up to protect its people from external influence. Ultimately, it would be this fundamental schizophrenia and continued ambivalence toward the demands of NGOs for effective access and monitoring capacities that would effectively lead to the closure of U.S. NGO operations in North Korea. Another important factor was that much greater levels of assistance delivered through the relatively less intrusive channel of the UN World Food Program (WFP) made the WFP the DPRK's preferred interlocutor.

In addition to the inevitable obstacles accompanying the establishment of unprecedented relationships inside the DPRK, the political and security environment surrounding the peninsula added further layers of difficulty to the relationship. The DPRK nuclear program, the DPRK missile program, submarine incidents, incidents along the Demilitarized Zone (DMZ), and naval clashes are only a few of the issues that directly influenced the working environment as NGOs sought to assess and address the needs of North Korean victims of natural and man-made disasters. Often, the DPRK view of NGO activities was negatively influenced by political events, and politics, in turn, shaped U.S., South Korean, and international public attitudes toward the situation in North Korea.

Despite repeated official claims to the contrary, U.S. humanitarian aid to North Korea became deeply entangled with ongoing political negotiations between the two governments. While the process of offering "food for talks" provided a means of advancing U.S.-DPRK dialogue—in form, if not in function—the effect of the politicization of aid was to greatly limit the negotiating leverage and relative influence of NGOs attempting to establish themselves in North Korea. Furthermore, politicization of food assistance confused North Korean officials, who already lacked a fundamental understanding of the nature, role, and intent of NGOs. Ultimately, the link between politics and NGO donations would be poisonous to NGO independence and would cost credibility and the ability to directly negotiate access for those NGOs most directly involved with bilateral provision of food assistance from the U.S. government; namely, the members of the Private Voluntary Organization Consortium (PVOC).

At the peak of the DPRK food crisis, the country's leadership allowed an unprecedented number of NGOs to work with and in the DPRK, but it also took extraordinary measures to protect its population from the dangerous influence of outsiders. While not all NGOs were directly involved inside North Korea, approximately 130 organizations worldwide participated in the humanitarian response to the DPRK food crisis at some point during the humanitarian response effort. Of this number, approximately 30 were U.S. NGOs. (*See text box on p.18 for a partial list.*) With such a large number of organizations involved, there was a presumption that the window into North Korea was being pried open wider than ever before. Between monitoring food distribution, wrestling with the DPRK bureaucracy, and exploring expanded activities in the fields of agriculture, medicine, and development, NGO interaction with the DPRK was potentially significant. However, as might be anticipated, NGO efforts have paled in comparison with efforts led by government and international organizations, which have been significantly larger in scale and scope. Furthermore, the lack of experience of most U.S. NGOs in dealing with North Korea, the relative success of the DPRK government's efforts to limit and control NGO activities within North Korea, and the continuously difficult political and security environment all served to impede NGO efforts and capacity to work effectively in North Korea.

INITIAL ENTRY INTO NORTH KOREA:
TERMS, CONDITIONS, AND OBSTACLES

U.S. NGOs had little or no experience in dealing with North Koreans and faced an unprecedented dearth of information about the DPRK's internal situation. In contrast to the experiences of NGOs elsewhere in the world—where representatives had either the relative freedom of movement and action that comes with anarchy or an established infrastructure of religious, social, or international organizations through which to work—the initial challenge in North Korea was not a logistical challenge but rather the political challenge of steering through the political barriers to working inside the country.

Since the end of the Korean War, the DPRK has lived up to the traditional moniker of the Korean Peninsula, the "Hermit Kingdom." It was, and is, arguably the most closed and inscrutable regime on earth. There has, however, been some limited contact between the North and the South, as well as some activities and exchanges carried out by scholars and Korean Americans. Much of the early contact in the humanitarian sphere took place between Korean Americans with either religious motivations or familial ties to North Korea. For example, a small group of Korean-American physicians began visiting North Korea in 1989 under the auspices of the Christian Association for Medical Mission (CAMM). Dr. Pilju Kim Joo, an agronomist at the University of Minnesota, has worked with the DPRK Academy of Social Sciences on numerous agriculture-related projects for more than a decade. Because the tragedy of the division of the Korean Peninsula extends to many individuals in the Korean-American community, a common subtext for visits to North Korea has been a desire to seek out long-lost relations. While there has been some variation, most of these exchanges have required—in a foreshadowing of what would be required of the broader NGO community— significant monetary or resource contributions in return for specialized and very controlled access to relatives. In addition to such ethnic links, there have been some

**PARTIAL LIST OF U.S. NONGOVERNMENTAL ORGANIZATIONS
INVOLVED IN OR WITH THE DPRK**

Adventist Development Relief Agency (ADRA)
American Friends Service Committee (AFSC)
American Aid
Amigos Internacionales
American National Council of Churches
Cooperative for Assistance and Relief Everywhere, Inc. (CARE)
Catholic Relief Services (CRS)
Christian Association for Medical Mission (CAMM)
Christian Friends of Korea
Children's Home Society of Minnesota
Church World Service (CWS)
Eugene Bell Centennial Foundation (EBCF)
Feed the Children
Food for the Hungry International (FHI)
Heifer Project International
Holt International Children's Services
InterAction
International Aid
Korean American Presbyterians (KAP)
Korean American Sharing Movement (KASM)
Latter-day Saints Charities (LDSC)
Mercy Corps International (MCI)
Nautilus Institute for Sustainable Development
Private Voluntary Organization Consortium (PVOC)
Samaritan's Purse
Southern Baptists
The Asia Foundation
United Methodist Committee on Relief (UMCOR)
U.S. Fund for UNICEF
World Summit Council (WSC)
World Vision International (WVI)

other scholarly exchanges and limited cooperation with the UN following North Korean membership in 1992. Despite such contacts, however, to most international and U.S. NGOs, North Korea has been a black hole.

Ignorance on the U.S. NGO side was amplified by deep North Korean suspicions of outsiders and the North Korean officials' resistance to permitting individuals who spoke or understood Korean to participate in NGO or other humanitarian activities. A virtual precondition to humanitarian work in North Korea, therefore, was an inability to communicate, especially with average North Koreans. This was early evidence of DPRK officials' concern that the North Korean populace should not be "contaminated" by outside influences. The effect of this prohibition on Korean language skills was that visitors to the DPRK were totally dependent on their interlocutors for information and interaction with counterparts. Even those NGOs able to operate relatively independently were unable to capture their own information about North Korea. Moreover, even if those rare foreigners with some Korean language ability should encounter an "average" North Korean, not only would they be unlikely to learn any useful information, but their efforts to make such contact would quickly be reported back to the authorities, since average North Koreans are obliged to report contacts with foreigners to the authorities. Frequent visitors to Pyongyang who escaped the confines of the government guesthouse or the Koryo Hotel reported that their DPRK "minders" knew details of their "independent and free" activities around the center of Pyongyang before they could get back to their hotels.

Unprecedented Opening: The Floods of August 1995

Before the flooding that hit North Korea in August 1995, it was inconceivable that North Korea would turn to the international community for assistance, particularly in an area as politically sensitive as food aid. The fundamental compromise inherent in the DPRK's decision to do so should not be taken lightly. The North had long been the recipient of assistance from the Soviet Union and China, but such aid had always been on North Korean terms and, perhaps more important, had implied no failure on North Korea's part.

Even before the flooding in 1995, North Korea had been suffering considerable food shortages[2] as a result of a lack of arable land, inefficiencies in its agricultural system, inevitable bottlenecks in its distribution system, further deterioration of its aging physical infrastructure, and, perhaps most important, the broader decline of its overall economy.[3] By the early 1990s, the DPRK government, presumably in response to the numerous signs of a growing food shortage, launched a campaign urging its citizens to eat only two meals a day, and there were a number of reports about food riots in North Korea.

A modern proverb heard in Pyongyang is *"Sanopi salaya nongopi sanda"* or "Industry must live for agriculture to live." Indeed, the DPRK agricultural system was extremely dependent upon the broader DPRK economy, which was in a freefall during most of the 1990s. As might be expected, the precipitous decline in DPRK agricultural production closely mirrored the overall decline of the DPRK economy.

Not only is DPRK agriculture extremely dependent on industrial inputs—North Korean farmers were reported to have some of the highest ratios of chemical fertilizer application in the world in the 1980s—but the collapse of key energy inputs into the economy directly affected field preparation, fertilizer production and distribution, irrigation, and harvesting. Thus, the DPRK agriculture system was vulnerable well before the floods of August 1995.[4] Flooding is a traditional problem on the Korean Peninsula during the late summer monsoon season. The floods of 1995 were worsened by agricultural practices that cultivated steep hillsides, left denuded forests, and otherwise contributed to the sedimentation and raising of the nation's river bottoms. There remains considerable debate about the exact extent and nationwide significance of the flooding during that year; however, the political ramifications of this particular disaster quickly became clear.

One key difference between the 1995 floods and previous floods was the North Korean response. The "Great Leader," Kim Il Sung, had died the previous July, and, in the form of the October 1994 Geneva Agreed Framework, North Korea had taken a tentative step toward normalizing its relations with the United States. Having joined the United Nations three years earlier, North Korea issued a formal appeal to the United Nations in September 1995. By October 1995, the UN WFP had opened an office in Pyongyang, and NGOs were not far behind.

Actors: Defining Characteristics within the NGO Community

The many types of NGOs and their relationships with national governments range from very close to quite distant and even antagonistic. For the purposes of understanding U.S. NGO interaction with North Korea, this study covers the activities of private organizations participating directly or indirectly in the provision of humanitarian aid, assistance, or development. Distinctions among NGOs may derive from differences in funding sources, organizational missions, or operational strategies. These organizations may raise funds directly through public appeals, or they may be far more institutionalized, with considerable resources. Some NGOs are essentially "food contractors" that provide delivery capacity for the U.S. government, while others seek to coordinate resources from both private sources and government. Yet another grouping includes denomination-specific religious NGOs, whose primary resource base is their own membership.

In the case of North Korea, the various types of NGOs sought to respond to North Korean food shortages through the following funding mechanisms:

- *Public campaigns:* Humanitarian aid organizations that relied on media campaigns to engender public sympathy and solicit donations through appeals to the public had a difficult time dealing with North Korea. The DPRK was very sensitive about its international image and treated attempts to portray images of starving children, and so on, as a national embarrassment. The result was a catch-22 for these NGOs, whose publicity efforts were opposed by a North Korean government that tried to show just enough distress to convince a suspicious community of the need while hiding the harshest realities of the crisis.

- *Conveyance NGOs:* These organizations coordinate closely with the U.S. government and often rely on the government for funding or supplies as administrators of U.S. government grants. The lack of real negotiating leverage with the DPRK led the U.S. government to "unofficially" link food aid with North Korean actions and even with specific negotiations. The result was that by the time U.S. government donations reached NGOs for distribution in North Korea, such assistance had already been "paid for" by the DPRK, thus depriving the NGOs of any real negotiating leverage on the ground.

• *Religious NGOs:* A third community involved organizations whose roots and resources were typically tied to religious organizations or beliefs. While generally smaller in scope, such organizations were frequently able to negotiate more effectively with the DPRK and respond more directly to needs as they arose, because they implemented their programs apart from political considerations and did not draw media attention to their efforts.

While not exhaustive, a summary list of the total food aid donated by U.S. NGOs engaged in North Korea can be found in Table 1.[5] Table 2 shows the comparative amount of food aid from government and NGO sources. Table 3 shows donations to North Korea by region. Over the course of the five-year period in question, government-provided food aid accounted for 88.2 percent of the total, whereas NGO-supplied food aid amounted to only 11.8 percent.[6] These charts do not list a number of other NGOs that, while not involved in the provision of food aid, were active in providing medicine, medical equipment, training, energy, and so on.

In the initial stages of the international response to the North Korean famine, one common refrain was that the DPRK was "not Africa." This was as true physically as it was politically. The food crisis in North Korea was largely systemic, although conditions were worsened by natural disasters.[7] Due to political controls on access within the DPRK, as well as DPRK sensitivity about showing the worst cases, the North Korean famine was not nearly as visible as the famines in Africa. North Korea did not suffer from a debilitating extended drought, but rather from crop failures, flooding, and food and water shortages that exacerbated distribution inequities caused by transportation bottlenecks inside North Korea. During the worst of the food crisis, the DPRK maintained remarkably strict controls over travel and access, although refugee flows to northeastern China did constitute a safety valve and escape route for those North Koreans able to find their way across the border. The challenging physical terrain and lack of transportation infrastructure limited the movement of people, particularly those weakened by hunger. The result was what aid workers soon came to call a "silent famine," reminiscent of the horrific famine in China that was estimated to have claimed nearly 30 million victims following the excesses of China's Great Leap Forward[8] in the late 1950s and early 1960s.

Perversely, the relative control maintained by the DPRK government meant that in times of shortage and deprivation, North Koreans had few viable alternatives and thus had incentive to be more rather than less loyal to the regime. The only way to survive was to find ways to move closer to the center, because the danger was that if one was too low on the priority list for distribution, there was no hope for survival. North Korea's strict political control also meant that for the international community desiring to assist North Korea there was no option but to work with and, in some cases, through the DPRK government. Ironically, the international aid community's reliance upon official government distribution mechanisms likely encouraged and enforced loyalty to the regime.

Table 1:
U.S. NGO Food Aid to DPRK 1996–2001 (Metric Tons M/T)

NGO	1996	1997	1998	1999	2000	2001	TOTAL
Archer Daniels Midland	-0-	-0-	327	-0-	-0-	-0-	327
Children's Home Service	-0-	-0-	-0-	-0-	36	35	71
Church World Service	-0-	1,676	113	-0-	-0-	61	1,850
Food for the Hungry International	-0-	255	-0-	-0-	-0-	-0-	255
Feed the Children	180	-0-	-0-	-0-	-0-	-0-	180
Korean-American Sharing Movement	-0-	5,211	-0-	-0-	-0-	-0-	5,211
Korean-American Presbyterians	-0-	-0-	360	-0-	-0-	-0-	360
Latter-day Saints Charities	80	-0-	180	-0-	1,000	-0-	1,260
Mercy Corps International	50	19	-0-	-0-	-0-	-0-	69
Southern Baptists	160	-0-	-0-	-0-	-0-	-0-	160
United Methodist Committee on Relief	-0-	300	-0-	-0-	-0-	-0-	300
World Summit Council	-0-	868	-0-	-0-	-0-	-0-	868
World Vision International	1,640	1,040	31	-0-	-0-	-0-	2,711
SUBTOTAL	**2,110**	**9,369**	**1,011**	**-0-**	**1,036**	**96**	**13,622**

Source: UN World Food Program

Table 2:
Total Food Aid to DPRK by Source 1996–2001 (Metric Tons M/T)

	1996	1997	1998	1999	2000	2001	TOTAL
Government Food Aid	779.3	464.25	747.1	823.0	888.2	971.1	4,673,500
NGO Food Aid	65.2	185.6	260.1	26.0	48.9	39.6	625,400
TOTAL	**844.5**	**649.8**	**1,007.2**	**849.0**	**937.1**	**1,011.3**	**5,298,900**

Source: UN World Food Program

Table 3:
U.S. Food Aid to North Korea by Region 1996–2001 (Metric Tons M/T)

Food Aid Source:	Government	NGO	Total	% of Global Total
Four Powers:				
USA	1,322,300 (28.3%)	12,024	1,334,324	25.2
ROK	789,700 (16.9%)	292,289	1,081,989	20.3
Japan	701,800 (15.0%)	2,095	703,895	13.3
China	618,500 (13.2%)	-0-	618,500	11.7
SUBTOTAL	3,432,300 (73.4%)	306,408	3,738,708	70.5
Europe	720,960 (15.4%)	261,065	982,025	18.5
Middle East	370,150 (7.9%)	-0-	370,150	7.0
South/ Southeast Asia	120,100 (2.6%)	9,417	129,517	2.2
North America (excluding U.S.)	29,800 (0.6%)	48,500	78,300	1.5
TOTAL	4,673,310 (99.9%)	625,390	5,298,700	99.7

Source: UN World Food Program

This is not to say that there was not a problem with displaced populations or refugees in North Korea. But compared with the more wide-scale and public movements in famines that have taken place in Africa and elsewhere, the signs that usually attract attention among NGOs and in the media were harder to pick up in North Korea. In fact, at the peak of the North Korean food shortages in late 1996 and through 1997, there were consistent reports of internal refugees within North Korea and external refugee flows into China. As might be anticipated, a review of a map of the areas in North Korea hardest hit by the famine shows an inverse relationship to the quality of the transportation infrastructure.[9] The transportation controls within the DPRK were as much a result of the regime's failure as part of its efforts at controlling population movements. Either way, it was those with the least access to the transportation infrastructure who suffered most and had the least opportunity to vote with their feet.

The limitations of the DPRK transportation infrastructure also served to limit the access of aid workers to the hardest-hit populations. For reasons both political and logistical, DPRK officials shielded foreign visitors from the worst of their people's suffering, while struggling to make sure that they were exposed to sufficient suffering in the less hard-hit areas to engender sympathy and support for continued aid flows. Despite limited and tightly controlled site visits, the vast majority of NGO delegations were limited to specific geographical areas and often were taken to the same sites outside Pyongyang over and over again. In retrospect, Pyongyang was the worst possible vantage point from which to gauge the famine's severity.

DPRK government involvement in all aspects of humanitarian relief posed a major challenge for NGOs—prima facie evidence of the low levels of mutual understanding and trust. The DPRK was regarded by NGOs as an anachronistic communist dictatorship not to be believed. Likewise, the DPRK had precious little experience in dealing with the outside world, particularly with organizations that purported to be "nongovernmental," a concept totally alien to the North Korean system and practice. From a North Korean perspective, anything "organized" had to be sanctioned, if not supported, by the government. The close coordination between some NGOs and the U.S. government, in addition to the role of some NGOs in conveying and monitoring U.S. government food aid, reinforced this impression. Hence, NGOs operating in North Korea had to deal with a DPRK regime that considered them a Trojan horse at worst and spies at best.

Likewise, U.S. distrust of the DPRK regime made verification of both DPRK claims of need and the distribution of food within North Korea a political necessity. Verification of this sort is an essential part of any effective humanitarian relief effort. However, verification required monitoring and unprecedented access to the North Korean countryside. To this day, the issue remains one of the primary sources of contention between DPRK officials and donors from the UN and NGO communities. In the 1990s, NGO workers were accustomed to making inspections on demand, but DPRK officials insisted on allowing area visits only with prior notification and approval. Despite resistance on North Korea's part, political and donor pressures in the United States (partially driven by concerns of possible diversion of humanitarian aid to the DPRK military) reinforced demands for monitoring. However, from the perspective of officials in Pyongyang, most U.S. NGOs were not conveying sufficient quantities of aid to justify such access. Furthermore, those NGOs conveying assistance as part of the PVOC projects had little leverage, as the political deals for the aid had already been made at a governmental level.

Phases of Engagement

The DPRK issued its first formal appeal for international assistance in September 1995. By October 1995, the UN WFP had established an office in Pyongyang. Other international organizations, including UNICEF (the UN Children's Fund), followed in fall 1995. North Korea Flood Relief, headed by former *Newsweek* correspondent Bernard Krisher, was one of the first U.S.-based NGOs established for North Korea. It began an Internet campaign to increase awareness of flood victims and solicit donations in fall 1995. This NGO is note-worthy because it was the first to employ the Internet in its public awareness strategy. By February 1996, U.S. NGOs (represented by Mercy Corps, Latter-day Saints Charities [LSDC], and World Vision) had visited North Korea. No sooner had individual NGOs begun interaction with the DPRK than it become apparent that a more coordinated effort would be required, given the level of political advo-cacy likely to be required in both Pyongyang and Washington.

The Formation of the InterAction North Korea Working Group

The dearth of information on and experience in North Korea motivated NGOs to pursue greater levels of consultation and coordination. Recalling this initial period of NGO engagement with North Korea, former World Vision vice presi-dent and current administrator of the U.S. Agency for International Development (USAID) Andrew Natsios noted that the sharing among NGOs of internal assess-ments and trip reports related to North Korea perhaps exceeded that of "any other crisis in the post-Cold War era."[10]

By spring 1996, a process of coordination and information exchange was initi-ated, largely through the Washington, D.C., headquarters of InterAction—a consortium of more than 150 U.S.-based NGOs. Much of this exchange was coor-dinated through the office of retired ambassador Jim Bishop, who was in charge of InterAction's disaster response division. In addition to providing NGOs with a venue for discussion and planning, InterAction began to serve a coordinating function. Even more important in this case, the core InterAction members formed the North Korea Working Group that began the process of advocacy to political and humanitarian aid communities that remained confused, if not skeptical, about the nature and severity of the need in North Korea.

The initial U.S. NGOs represented on the Executive Committee of the North Korea Working Group included Adventist Development and Relief Agency International (ADRA), American Friends Service Committee (AFSC), Catholic Relief Services (CRS), Church World Service (CWS), Heifer Project International, Holt International Children's Services, International Aid, LDSC, Mercy Corps International (MCI), United Methodist Committee on Relief (UMCOR), and the U.S. Fund for UNICEF.

Since InterAction had a close institutional relationship with USAID, the members of the North Korea Working Group played an important role in urging the U.S. government to focus on and eventually respond to the North Korean food shortages in early 1996.

The Role of the Food Aid Liaison Unit

One effort of InterAction's North Korea Working Group was to support the formation of the Food Aid Liaison Unit (FALU) in Pyongyang. One of the most difficult challenges facing NGOs was the DPRK's resistance to an ongoing or resident NGO presence in North Korea, so the FALU's intended purpose was to facilitate communication between member NGOs—regardless of nationality— and the North Korean government's Flood Damage Rehabilitation Committee (FDRC). The DPRK had established the FDRC shortly after the August 1995 floods as an interagency committee to deal with all foreign NGOs, except those from South Korea and Japan. Although available to U.S. NGOs, over the course of its tenure in Pyongyang, the FALU served primarily Canadian and European NGOs, as well as the Hong Kong–based Catholic relief charity Caritas. In general, the authorized channel of communication between NGO representatives from Korea or Japan and North Koreans was the Asia Pacific Peace Committee (APPC) of the Korea Workers Party.

With a resident office in Pyongyang, the FALU provided support to nonresident NGOs seeking to participate in the response to North Korea's food shortage and monitored the distribution of food aid in North Korea. For practical reasons, as well as better coordination with other participants in the international humanitarian effort, the FALU attached itself to the WFP office in Pyongyang. The FALU advised food donors about the areas of greatest need, both nutritionally and geographically; monitored aid distributions; and provided reports to donor organizations. Beginning with a staff of two in fall 1996, the FALU grew to a staff of 20 international monitors temporarily resident in Pyongyang and had some degree of access to 158 of North Korea's 211 counties. Thus, the FALU had a synergistic relationship with the WFP, with FALU representatives providing the WFP with additional monitoring resources and the WFP making available its growing access to the North Korean countryside. The FALU's founding members were:

• ACT – Action by Churches Together (Geneva, Switzerland)

- ADRA – Adventist Development and Relief Agency (Silver Spring, Maryland and Geneva, Switzerland)
- Caritas – Catholic Church funded global relief agency, based in Rome but supported with contributions from Japan and Hong Kong
- CFGB – Canadian Foodgrains Bank (Winnipeg, Canada)
- MCI – Mercy Corps International (Portland, Oregon)
- WVI – World Vision International (Monrovia, California)

Eventually, PMU InterLife of Sweden, the Cooperative for Assistance and Relief Everywhere, Inc. (CARE) of Germany and the United States, the Taize Community of France, and others would contribute to the FALU.

Despite the efforts of FALU representatives in Pyongyang, some NGO representatives viewed the FALU's very creation as another premature concession to the NGOs' inability to perform independent monitoring in North Korea and to the DPRK officials' preference for handling the monitoring and distribution of food through more easily manipulated, on-the-ground international organizations such as the WFP, which formed an early preference for the Public Distribution System (PDS) as the vehicle for managing food aid distribution efforts.

Musgrove Conferences and International NGO Consultation

As the situation unfolded on the ground in North Korea, InterAction's North Korea Working Group began to push for greater coordination and cooperation from NGOs. One result was a conference on North Korea that subsequently became known as Musgrove I, held in November 1996 on the historic Musgrove Plantation in Georgia. Some 75 representatives from NGOs, government agencies, and international aid organizations attended this conference. As might be expected given the topic, the conference brought to light many differing and competing views of the situation in North Korea and recommendations on how best to respond. One of the fundamental challenges was the difficulty of dealing with the North Korean crisis from afar and the NGOs' consequent desire to establish an on-the-ground presence in the country. The decision of some of the conference's leading organizers to designate a representative NGO "coordinator" who would be resident in Pyongyang proved to be particularly controversial. While some saw real utility in having a unified presence on the ground, others saw the move as playing into the hands of the DPRK desire to limit the number of on-the-ground NGO representatives. In the end, the result in part of DPRK opposition to a U.S. representative and candidates with Korean language capability, it was an experienced Canadian, Erich Weingartner, who accepted the position as head of the FALU.

The conference's primary focus was the establishment of a loose coalition to prevent or relieve a looming famine in North Korea. However, other issues discussed at the meeting also continued to be issues of debate among NGOs, including the extent to which the DPRK PDS should be relied upon and the extent to which NGOs should push for the inclusion of Korean-speaking aid workers and monitors. The decision to bend to the North Korean demand that resident aid workers in Pyongyang not include Korean Americans or Korean language speakers proved to be particularly controversial. The participation of U.S. government officials in the meeting also introduced what was soon to become one of the defining issues of NGO involvement in North Korea: the U.S. government's proclivity to use food aid as a carrot to entice the DPRK into talks.

The recognition of the political elements of the North Korea question was not entirely one-sided. Given the political environment in Washington, the NGOs and other participants at Musgrove quickly recognized the need to publicize the crisis and put pressure on both the Clinton administration and Congress to act before it was too late. In specific recognition of this need, a further outgrowth of the increasingly collaborative effort among NGOs was the creation of the "Stop the Famine Committee" in March 1997. With a membership composed of many of the NGOs represented at Musgrove and others, the committee launched a focused television advertising campaign consisting of three ads broadcast in the Washington, D.C., area in April 1997. While there were many other factors, by June 1997 food shortages in the DPRK had become a focus of the major U.S. news outlets, and by July 1997 the Clinton administration significantly increased its pledges of food aid to North Korea.

Such coordination continued, and a subsequent meeting, sometimes referred to as Musgrove II, was convened in fall 1997. The participation was expanded to include European, South Korean, and Japanese organizations in the coordination process. Following a less formal effort in Seoul in 1998, a fourth conference was convened in Beijing in May 1999 that, for the first time, included Chinese institutions and organizations. Such gatherings had become a venue for identifying areas of common concern and publicly urging the appropriate authorities to take action to address these issues. In what had become almost a mantra of the aid community, many of the participants at the Beijing conference voiced concerns that the North Korean government was not complying with international standards to ensure that assistance reached the most needy, was not allowing adequate access to vulnerable groups, and was continuing to require prearranged monitoring visits.

Japanese NGOs, long isolated from South Korean and American NGOs in their efforts to aid North Korea, eagerly hosted the 2000 International NGO Conference on North Korea in Tokyo, Japan, in June 2000. In concert with dramatic developments in North-South political relations, South Korean NGOs moved to assume leadership of the international NGO effort in North Korea by hosting the 2001 International NGO Conference on North Korea in Seoul, Korea. At the conclusion of the Seoul conference, participants "strongly endorsed" the South Korean government's policy of engagement with North Korea, commended the European Union's efforts to provide humanitarian assistance, and urged the U.S. and Japanese governments to continue their aid. The NGOs also urged the North Korean government to allow greater access to the North Korean people. By the time of these two conferences, however, the immediacy of the food crisis had faded, as had many NGOs' fervor for directly engaging the North. As a result, the meetings had been transformed from small, action-oriented strategy sessions to larger consultative conferences more concerned with policy issues and political support for the most recent diplomatic developments to engage North Korea.

Creation of the Private Voluntary Organization Consortium

Another outgrowth of the collaborative process begun in InterAction was the formation of a formal NGO consortium with support from the U.S. government. The U.S. PVOC was formed in June 1997. Its original members were Amigos Internacionales, CARE, CRS, Mercy Corps, and World Vision. The group was expanded in March 1999 to include ADRA, the Carter Center, CWS, the Korean American Sharing Movement (KASM), and LDSC. USAID contracted first CRS and then CARE to manage the consortium. USAID's Office of Foreign Disaster Assistance and the U.S. Department of Agriculture (USDA) funded the consortium's activities with grants that eventually totaled approximately $4.5 million and material aid (food and medicine) worth $55 million.

The U.S. government's decision to support the creation of the consortium was at least in part motivated by a desire to have U.S. NGOs distribute and monitor a portion of the U.S. food aid that had previously been donated primarily through the WFP. The motivation for NGOs to collaborate so closely with the U.S. government is less certain, but it likely had to do primarily with a need for resources in addressing a crisis for which there was little public sympathy and even less financial support. Other factors may have included the need for getting into a North Korea that had continued to resist NGO efforts to establish an on-the-ground presence in Pyongyang.

Despite an apparent outward commonality in mission, there was an underlying tension among the PVOC membership, the result in part of the distrust that mainstream NGOs felt toward Amigos Internacionales, a Southern Baptist-related aid organization with strong ties to the office of Senator Jesse Helms (R-NC). (It was hinted that the inclusion of Amigos Internacionales in the PVOC was a precondition for Senator Helms to allow USAID to provide funding for this operation.)

The PVOC's primary official objectives were to monitor the receipt and distribution of U.S. government food aid in North Korea and to provide food to unemployed farm and factory workers living in urban areas where factories were closed or underutilized. In particular, while in North Korea, PVOC members would:

• Assess and approve food-for-work projects in collaboration with the FDRC at the national and local levels.

• Monitor the progress of work against plans developed by the county governments and on which the food allocation was based.

- Verify the delivery of food to the county warehouses and/or public distribution centers, witness the distribution of food from public distribution centers, and verify that workers received food for the work they completed.

- Work closely with WFP staff, who provided logistical support for the receipt and distribution of food from port to county warehouse.

Between August 1997 and June 2000, the PVOC implemented five projects, one involving medical supplies and four involving food distributed as part of the Food for Work (FFW) project.

- **Stage I – August 1997 to November 1997:** A five-member PVOC team monitored distribution of 55,000 metric tons of U.S. government-purchased grain. A quarter of the grain was allocated to FFW programs.

- **Stage II – February 1998 to August 1998:** Three non-American medical professionals representing the PVOC oversaw distribution of a $5 million Office of Disaster Assistance project. Under the auspices of UNICEF, drugs and medical supplies were distributed to children's institutions and pediatric hospitals.

- **Stage III – June 1998 to October 1998:** An eight-member American team from the PVOC monitored distribution of 75,000 metric tons of grain for FFW projects.

- **Stage IV – February 1999 to July 1999:** Another eight-member PVOC team monitored 75,000 metric tons of FFW grain.

- **Stage V – July 1999 to May 2000, "The Potato Project":** Food aid totaling 100,000 metric tons was programmed to support FFW projects and a separate potato project that involved the planting of 1,000 tons of potato seed. This phase involved the first direct bilateral[11] food aid program between the United States and North Korea. The previous four phases had been conducted in conjunction with UN agencies.

PVOC Waterloo: The Potato Project

The PVOC's final project in North Korea was arguably its most innovative, most political, and ultimately most controversial. It also marked the greatest blurring of the lines between government and NGO, as well as between humanitarian aid and politics. In April 1999, the United States, the DPRK, and the PVOC signed a three-party agreement under which the PVOC, through its own seed potatoes, and the U.S. government, through the PVOC, agreed to provide a further 100,000 metric tons of emergency food aid, again in support of the FFW projects. Though not officially linked, this three-party agreement and the provision of U.S. food aid that was not conveyed specifically through the WFP were widely considered to have been compensation[12] for the DPRK agreement to allow U.S. inspectors access to the suspect underground facilities at Kumchang-ri, which had been a thorn in U.S.-DPRK relations since the existence of the facilities was made public in August 1998.

The Potato Project was beset by both internal and external difficulties and was terminated after only one year, leaving the PVOC in shambles. By all accounts, the PVOC mobilized rapidly to purchase and plant the seed potatoes, despite getting a very late start. The monitoring of and follow-up for the project, however, apparently fell victim to PVOC management and staffing problems, as well as to reported disputes among the core members of the PVOC leadership. These difficulties were compounded by a typhoon that scuttled most of the anticipated potato crop, and ultimately the PVOC program coordinators, CARE and CRS, which had administered the FFW program, opted to pull out of the PVOC.

According to a detailed U.S. General Accounting Office (GAO) report on the project, the "U.S. Agency for International Development said the bilateral assistance project seemed to demonstrate that the North Korean government was not yet ready to engage in a way that would support success."[13] Others who were directly involved in the project's implementation put the blame more squarely on the shoulders of the PVOC management team.[14] While there appears to be plenty of blame to go around, the result was the cessation of bilateral U.S. aid, the withdrawal of the PVOC presence from Pyongyang, and a significant curtailment of any effort to coordinate the efforts of NGOs and the U.S. government. This GAO report was but one example of the political sensitivities surrounding NGO activities in North Korea.

Reasons for NGO Pullout/Departure

On April 4, 2000, CARE—one of the leading members of the PVOC—announced through a press release of a statement by CARE president Peter Bell that effective June 30, 2000, it was withdrawing from the PVOC and ceasing its activities in the DPRK. Bell stated that "CARE believes now is the appropriate time for the organization to move in the direction of sustainable rehabilitation and development programs in North Korea." He continued, "For such programs to be effectively and efficiently implemented, however, it is necessary for CARE to have significantly higher levels of access to people in need than it does currently." The release concluded that "Despite a nearly four-year dialogue with the North Korean government regarding the importance of access, transparency, and accountability,…the operational environment in North Korea has not progressed to a point where CARE feels it is possible to implement effective rehabilitation programs."[15]

Somewhat ironically, the NGOs that have been the most successful in North Korea over the long term appear to have been the smaller, religious-affiliated NGOs that have generally steered clear of political entanglements and focused instead on ongoing "niche" programs. The Eugene Bell Centennial Foundation (EBCF), LDSC, AFSC, ADRA, and others have all been able to maintain some type of engagement with the DPRK. While each of these groups has its distinct interests and motives, these organizations have not pushed for a permanent presence on the ground in North Korea, have been content with a slower pace of engagement with the DPRK (perhaps befitting their capacity), and have built relationships over time at both the central and local levels in North Korea.

SECTOR-SPECIFIC REVIEW OF U.S. NGO ACTIVITIES

The main thrust of NGO interaction with North Korea was in response to the North Korean appeal for immediate humanitarian assistance—primarily in the form of food and medicine—in the wake of flooding in August 1995. However, it quickly became apparent to most who approached North Korea that the food shortages and medical needs were chronic. Accordingly, most NGO interaction with the North remained focused on the strictly "humanitarian" sectors of providing food aid, medicine, and technical assistance in agricultural projects directly related to food production. The activities of NGOs were further constrained by three other factors—the limited capacity of NGO financial resources, U.S. government restrictions on government support for "development" projects with North Korea, and North Korea's own initial reluctance to accept anything other than food assistance.

As has been noted, DPRK officials did not clearly understand the nature of NGOs and from the beginning tended to have unrealistic expectations about the amount of assistance that NGOs—both individually and collectively—might provide. There is considerable evidence that NGO contributions were often weighed against the much larger contributions being made by individual donor governments and international organizations such as the WFP. The results of such expectations, often expressed in the form of DPRK demands for a minimum amount of aid that the DPRK would require before it would grant a visa for a visit to Pyongyang, were twofold. First, many NGOs quickly determined that they could not compete in the provision of grains or basic foodstuffs and began to seek out niche markets in both the agriculture and health sectors where they might make a smaller, if more direct, contribution. Second, this pressure might be presumed to have been an impetus behind the increasingly close collaboration between some NGOs and the U.S. government. However, as would rapidly become apparent, the conveyance and monitoring of U.S. government food aid did not necessarily result in increased influence for NGOs.

A select few NGOs were able, however, to find a niche in which they could operate beyond the Musgrove coordination process, gain access to the DPRK countryside beyond Pyongyang, and operate relatively independently of the broader political environment. While not immune to the pendulum swing of DPRK politics and international crises, NGOs such as the EBCF and the Nautilus Institute for Security and Sustainability, by focusing narrowly and consistently on relatively obscure projects, were able to successfully carry out efforts that continue to grow more important in substance and symbolism. The Nautilus Institute's wind-power project—setting up small wind-turbine generators in Unha-ri—has been a bright spot during many political downturns, and the EBCF's efforts to essentially adopt a major portion of the DPRK tuberculosis treatment center system is an example of the Christian mandate to help the helpless.

Food and Agriculture

Because the initial DPRK appeal was for food assistance, most of the first NGO respondents to the crisis—such as CRS, ADRA, LDSC, CWS, AFSC, and others—responded with token donations of emergency food and medical supplies. At the same time, the NGOs were quick to recognize their comparative disadvantage and limitations in the provision of basic food grains, so most shifted rapidly to more focused projects. For example, ADRA shipped powdered milk, rice, and medicine shortly after the 1995 appeal, then shifted its approach to set up and operate a bakery in Pyongyang. Similarly, the CWS refocused on setting up food production in North Korea.

Another way that NGOs adapted to the unique structure of the DPRK system was the "adoption" of particular collective farms or villages. For example, MCI adopted the Kumsong-ri collective farm through its agricultural rehabilitation and exchange program. This farm focused on orchards, and MCI was able to convey apple trees donated from the state of Oregon and other sources. LSDC, the Mennonite Central Committee (MCC), AFSC, and Amigos Internacionales have similarly assisted particular cooperative farms. ADRA sent a team of heart surgeons in 1996. As was typical, visiting delegations delivered gifts of medicines. In many cases, this "adoption process" was the price of access. DPRK dictated where help was needed and where NGOs were allowed to contribute.

The Korean-American church community was a major supporter of humanitarian relief activities in both the food and medical areas—through the formation of KASM, an active umbrella national group, and through more individualized private or unpublicized efforts focused on particular home regions or assigned areas such as the Rajin-Sonbong free trade area in the far northeastern part of North Korea. Many of these activities, including support for model farms and provision of supplies and equipment to form bakeries and noodle factories, were supported with logistics and supplies provided by local Chinese trading firms on the China-North Korea border.

It is difficult to capture the scale of the inputs provided by Korean-American religious groups via northeast China, but these activities have been some of the most consistent and substantial relief efforts to have proceeded continuously under the international aid community's radar screen and without overt official coordination via central authorities in Pyongyang. Estimates of the amount of assistance from Korean-American religious sources to operations inside North Korea in the area of agriculture or inputs to sustain bakeries and noodle factories may reach $10 million. These efforts grew over time to include provision of coats, shoes, and clothing for children and adults, and the provision of certain drugs and medicines, including major shipments of drugs by KASM. The estimated value of these additional efforts also reached into the millions of dollars.

One of the central staging points for some of these operations was the Yanbian University of Science and Technology in Yanji, China, an institution established by Dr. Kim Jin-kyung, a Korean American with deep ties to the Korean-American church community, as well as a range of financial supporters in South Korea who were also motivated to provide relief to both North Koreans inside the country and refugees who crossed the border seeking food in China. In some cases, the operations inside North Korea have relied on the good offices of local officials who have found themselves the responsible actors in their communities as the central government has declared that *juche* really means that the counties and provinces have no choice but to fend for themselves. In some cases, local officials and the cross-border relationships they established have not survived or have become targets of the central government as recovery has taken hold.

Health and Medicine

In some cases, early food relief was accompanied by much-needed medical supplies. Many NGOs have regularly included medicine and medical equipment in their periodic donations to the DPRK. MCI, LDSC, and many others have donated considerable quantities of both new and used medical equipment. Furthermore, CRS has worked with the DPRK Ministry of Public Health on many of its projects.

One remarkable example of a relatively small NGO's contribution has been the work of EBCF. After an early focus on providing immediate food aid in the form of corn shipped from China, EBCF identified the ultimate niche market in the form of the DPRK tuberculosis clinics. Since the DPRK does not officially recognize the existence of tuberculosis in North Korea, EBCF has been able to gradually build up its network of support in the country, has imported mobile diagnostic vans, is now treating some 30,000 North Korean patients, and regularly visits more than half of the nation's remote tuberculosis clinics.

Energy

While there have been some innovative efforts by ADRA[16] to supply the DPRK with solar kitchens for remote areas where access to electricity or fuel is particularly challenging, there has been little that NGOs could do to address one of the overarching problems facing the DPRK economy—severe energy shortages. Not only is the scope of this problem enormous, but it is also tied up in the politics surrounding the 1994 U.S.-DPRK Agreed Framework and the ongoing efforts to construct light-water nuclear reactors in exchange for the older model graphite nuclear reactors that North Korea shut down or ceased construction on in late 1994. The international consortium building these reactors—the New York–based Korean Peninsula Energy Development Organization (KEDO)—offers one of the most fascinating and far-reaching efforts to engage North Koreans in North Korea. However, its activities are hardly representative of those of NGOs.

Although not undertaken by a typical humanitarian-aid-providing NGO, one effort worth noting has been the U.S.-DPRK Village Wind Power Pilot Project of the Berkeley, California-based Nautilus Institute for Security and Sustainability. Like many of the agriculture projects, this effort has focused on a select village—

Unha-Ri in this case—and over the course of several years and several visits has set up a number of small wind turbines that now provide a significant portion of the electricity needs of the target village.[17]

Economic Development/Training/Capacity Building

As the NGO experience in North Korea has grown and as NGOs have attempted to move toward more development-focused programs, the need for various levels of familiarization tours and training has become apparent. Over the past five years, an unprecedented number of North Korean delegations have visited the United States, China, and other countries for training and site visits.[18] The AFSC, MCI, Carter Center, and many others have organized agricultural study tours to the United States. In a project run by lawyer and professor Jerome A. Cohen, the San Francisco-based Asia Foundation ran a groundbreaking series of training sessions in China on legal issues and supported the visit to the United States of various agriculture- and development-focused DPRK officials and experts. As part of its "Books for Asia" program, The Asia Foundation has provided almost 70,000 books since 1996; sponsored annual law seminars in Beijing from 1998 through 2001; and hosted agricultural, library science, and English as a second language delegations with representatives from leading Pyongyang-based universities and the Grand People's Study House. Over time and with consistent interaction, The Asia Foundation has been able to expand its relationships and de-link its activities from the U.S.-DPRK relationship— although there has been a limit on the number of people who can participate in training and the duration of the programs the foundation has been able to sponsor. Nevertheless, despite political obstacles, these programs have been successful in reaching some North Korean specialists and in broadening their experience and understanding of resources and methods available through sustained interaction with the outside world.

NORTH KOREA'S STRUCTURE AND PROCESS FOR HANDLING U.S. NGOS

If engagement with the DPRK proved a challenge for U.S. NGOs, conversely, the DPRK bureaucracy faced an even greater adjustment in its interactions with the United States. For decades, the DPRK has cultivated a deep mistrust of the outside world, particularly its archenemy, the United States. From a DPRK perspective, it was unlikely that NGOs were anything other than either Trojan horses intent on destroying the North Korean regime or intelligence-gathering tools of the U.S. intelligence community.

To understand how suspicious the DPRK must have been of the U.S. NGOs, one must understand how very tightly information is controlled in North Korea. The DPRK remains one of the most autarkic and secretive regimes in history. Even within North Korean society, information is generally shared on a need-to-know basis; there is little in the way of horizontal information sharing or government-level interagency coordination. Economic and health statistics, in particular, are generally regarded as state secrets and, even when released, are viewed as unreliable.

Table 4:
NGO Food Aid to DPRK 1996–2001 by Region

Percentage of Total NGO Food Aid to DPRK, Metric Tons (M/T)

Region	1996	1997	1998	1999	2000	2001	TOTAL	% of Total
South Korea	914	66,473	179,567	3,996	7,801	3,996	262,747	48.8%
Europe	57,994	107,439	60,234	12,000	21,291	2,107	261,065	48.4%
United States	2,110	8,501	1,281	-0-	1,036	96	13,024	2.4%
Japan	168	178	1,729	-0-	20	-0-	2,095	0.4%
SUB-TOTALS	61,186	182,591	242,811	15,996	30,148	6,199	538,931	100.0%

Source: UN World Food Program

Faced with an increasingly open and democratic society to the South, the DPRK has relied upon strict government control over the flow of information, the movement of people, and the means of production as important tools in the maintenance of its regime. Even as the socialist bloc has collapsed and former Asian socialist allies such as China have dramatically opened up, North Korea has gone to extremes to preserve its unprecedented level of control and limit the exposure of its citizenry to the polluting influences of the outside world.

One result of this level of suspicion and control was to greatly influence visiting NGO representatives' perceptions of the regime. In a number of cases, NGOs and other humanitarian organizations that approached North Korea with the intent of helping were converted into opponents of the regime and of aid provision in part because of the treatment they received at the hands of DPRK officials.

A Different Kind of Donor-Recipient Relationship

In contrast to the relative anarchy of providing aid in the context of failed systems, the DPRK regime has at times appeared to be the model of efficiency. Numerous early international officials and NGO representatives were amazed at the social order and relative functionality of state instruments such as the PDS.

Such regime capacity certainly helped maintain social order and facilitated transportation and distribution in a relatively smoother manner than was the case in societies without a functional government. However, with that efficiency came a degree of government control that placed real limits on where and when NGO representatives could travel, what type of activities they could pursue, and with whom they could interact.

After the initial shock of finding a country that was not typically "third world" wore off, NGO representatives quickly became frustrated as DPRK officials blocked some the most common monitoring devices, including morbidity tracking, nutritional surveys, market surveys, and price surveys. Perhaps most grating was the fact that even as the total amount of aid delivered increased and the time in country lengthened, international humanitarian officials and NGO representatives still had to negotiate and announce inspection and monitoring visits well in advance.

At the conclusion of a lengthy stay in North Korea, one UN official said of the PDS, "It's very efficient; I mean it works. But we are not naïve. We have 300 monitoring visits a month. They don't mean anything, because there are no random visits." Ultimately, such monitoring provided assurances on an institutional rather than an individual level. Through prearranged monitoring visits, it was possible to confirm that aid had reached a designated institution, but there was no way to monitor whom it reached within that institution. More important, individuals who were outside the institutional umbrella were not even on the distribution radar screen.

Paying for Visits

Another common difficulty for U.S. NGOs in particular was the difficulty of getting into North Korea. Since the United States does not have diplomatic relations with North Korea, obtaining a North Korean visa was a real challenge. NGO representatives would typically have to stop first in Beijing and hope that a visa would be waiting for them at the DPRK Embassy there. More significantly, approval for such visas on the North Korean side was not easily given. NGO representatives could not simply send a fact-finding mission to Pyongyang to decide whether or not to give aid. In fact, a Korean proverb often quoted by visitors—"*Bin sonulo omyon, andoinda*" or "One does not come with empty hands"—became the mantra for the host. Visiting delegations were expected, if not required, to bring at least token donations, and many NGOs timed their visits to the DPRK with the arrival of aid being shipped in to justify their visits in the eyes of Pyongyang. In some cases, DPRK officials were so demanding that NGOs felt they were "paying for visits with aid." The expectation was higher still for organizations hoping to establish a presence on the ground in North Korea.

Limiting Residence and Communication

As uncomfortable as DPRK officials were about visits by NGO representatives, they were even more suspicious of the NGO desire to set up shop in Pyongyang. As a result, the question of resident staff in North Korea became an issue for nearly every NGO hoping to establish a longer-term operation in North Korea. This was particularly true for U.S. citizens to whom, largely due to the politics of the day, DPRK officials nearly always refused to grant ongoing residency. Even once residency was established, it was not open-ended, and regular visits to China for a new visa were required. This renewal, too, often depended on ongoing levels of aid that DPRK officials could use to justify the presence of "barbarians" in the capital.

In addition to the "entrepreneurial" demands of FDRC officials for more aid as a justification to establish residency, many NGOs reported their impression that the Korean People's Army was the most uncomfortable with the presence of "hostile" foreigners on the ground and commonly pressured the FDRC to limit, if not reduce, the number of resident NGO representatives in Pyongyang.

Hard-Nosed Interlocutors

The NGO and humanitarian aid communities that saw themselves as largely altruistic were unprepared for the sometimes hostile stance and aggressive negotiating tactics of North Korean officials. Furthermore, humanitarian aid NGOs had no leverage because they could not credibly threaten to walk away and take their aid with them, particularly since the terms of delivery and amounts had already been negotiated between the U.S. and DPRK governments. Even those that were independent of the U.S. government could not walk away, usually because their religious ideals prevented them from abandoning their efforts to help the needy just because of their interlocutors' hostility. From this initial experience, some DPRK officials learned to hold their own populace hostage to their demands or conditions. In essence, the official DPRK response to NGO representatives was, "Do it our way or we won't allow you to help our people."

North Korean officials' desire that the country not be seen as impoverished, to save face and not be treated as "third world" meant that much of the aid given to North Korea was offensive to the North Korean leadership, if not unacceptable. Even clothing or medical equipment that was old but in otherwise good condition—and certainly better than much of what North Korea had on hand—often became an issue. As NGO contributions were often portrayed and received as gifts proffered by a visiting delegation—in North Korean eyes, in the same manner as official delegations to the Chinese imperial court came bearing gifts—the quality and presentation of these gifts came to represent the respect in which the court was held. Hence several NGO delegations reported encountering North Korean outrage and deep offense at receiving medical equipment that was usable but noticeably old or sloppily packaged.

Through these and many similar tactics, DPRK officials were successfully able to come across not as the beggar, but instead as the recipient of entreaties from the outside world. In contrast, the would-be donors, the NGOs, became the supplicants, asking the DPRK for the "privilege" of helping the North Korean people.

WHO IS IN CHARGE?: INSTITUTIONAL FRICTIONS WITHIN NORTH KOREA

Another source of confusion for NGOs in dealing with the DPRK has been the relatively opaque nature of the country's government. There are apparent turf battles among the FDRC, the Foreign Ministry, and the military. While the NGOs had little direct contact with the DPRK military, the Korean People's Army was a frequent bogeyman used to justify the inability of DPRK officials to organize visits, meetings, and so on. While the veracity of these claims is difficult to gauge, perhaps the DPRK officials were well versed in "good cop–bad cop" tactics, as these tactics were and continue to be an important factor in NGO efforts to engage DPRK officials.

Several NGOs observed that the ministries would quarrel over who had secured pledges of assistance and that they were very reluctant to allow contact with other ministries or organizations during the course of a visit to the DPRK. This is partially explained by a genuine lack of communication among DPRK government organs. An alternative explanation, however, is that the Ministry of Agriculture, the Ministry of Foreign Affairs, the Ministry of Health, and so on, were all competing—not only for access to the aid donated by the international community, but also for the credit and influence that might be gained internally for securing such aid. Despite the fact that the FDRC was purported to be an interagency creation, it quickly became a bureaucratic institution in its own right and joined the fray.

Local officials tended to accept NGOs much more readily and extend cooperation much more easily than officials on the national level. Not only were officials at the central level likely to be more politicized, they also had less immediate personal or local interest in the aid being delivered to the countryside. One European official quoted a DPRK deputy foreign minister as saying that the "DPRK is not really interested in NGOs and has accepted them until now because of the wishes of the donor countries."[19]

Yet another inhibiting factor involved constraints on the individual interlocutors between the NGOs and the DPRK government. NGOs reported a wide disparity of results depending on the quality and enthusiasm, or lack thereof, of their particular North Korean hosts. Such affiliations were also an issue for the individual North Koreans involved, as there was certainly a risk of being perceived as being "too close" or "too friendly" with representatives of the American imperialists.

Despite these and many other institutional obstacles within the North Korean bureaucracy, most of the NGOs that have remained engaged in North Korea over the long haul have observed a slow and fitful learning curve. Kathi Zellweger, a representative of Caritas International Hong Kong, who has made numerous trips to North Korea over the past decade, observed, "While the DPRK authorities have not fully accepted the concept of nongovernmental aid agencies operating on a long-term basis in their country, there is an understanding now that NGOs in many countries have a strong voice and thus can be quite influential." [20]

Tools for Quarantine

DPRK officials tasked with interacting with NGOs were given seemingly conflicting mandates: Get as much substantive assistance as possible, but limit the exposure of North Korea as much as possible. The initial DPRK response to this mandate was institutional; namely, to create or put forward organizations such as the FDRC or the PDS that would serve to limit the number of DPRK citizens with exposure to foreigners. A second strategy involved limiting the number of foreigners who could visit North Korea and restricting the ability of those who did make it into North Korea to travel or communicate.

Management of all external contacts through the FDRC provided an institutional buffer widely perceived by NGOs to be a further control mechanism. Almost invariably, NGOs that were invited to North Korea by the FDRC or otherwise assigned the FDRC as a principal interlocutor had a very difficult time "breaking out" of the FDRC track.

Similarly, DPRK officials' insistence that food aid be distributed through the PDS provided a vehicle for control over distribution of the resources provided by the international community, reinforcing the existing institutional, regional, and social biases of the North Korean system. International officials accustomed to operating in environments where there was little or no infrastructure were initially eager to work through the PDS. While some were deeply suspicious of the PDS and argued that its use would only serve to legitimize and "prop up" the DPRK government, others claimed to eschew politics and be concerned only with getting food to needy people as efficiently as possible. In fact, compared with the manner in which NGOs usually work in the context of humanitarian disasters, the PVOC structure itself was a significant concession to the North Korean need to maintain control. Though its intentions were the opposite, the PVOC structure played into North Korean preferences for a limited number of representatives who would be easier to control. Furthermore, the PVOC's unique structure—with different aspects of the projects being managed by different NGOs, all in a semi-collaborative relationship with the government—led to disagreements and, in some respects, poor management, particularly of the last PVOC mission.

Innocents Abroad

In discussing the many difficulties surrounding the treatment of NGOs by DPRK officials—the deep-seated DPRK suspicion of the outside world and the considerable efforts the DPRK made to limit NGO access and control exposure to outside influences—it is tempting to portray the challenges faced by NGOs as being one-sided. In fact, many of the problems NGOs faced were of their own making. NGO staff had little previous experience with Korean culture.

While NGOs were used to dealing with countries in chaos and government officials who had been humbled in some respect by their national failure, the average North Korean official remained, at least in public, fiercely defensive of the DPRK regime. DPRK officials maintained what many would consider an unjustified level of national pride, quickly taking offense at any treatment that suggested they were needy or underdeveloped. Thus, there was a heavy focus on materials rather than advice. This was particularly challenging for NGOs reared on the notion that "teach a man to fish and you will feed him for a lifetime." North Koreans insisted not only that they knew how to fish, but that Kim Il Sung had invented fishing! For DPRK officials who were embarrassed enough to be asking for aid, it was a matter of pride and respect.

U.S. NGOs quickly learned that their statements and activities outside the DPRK could not be separated from their activities in the DPRK. Nowhere was this clearer than in the activities of many NGOs along the Chinese border with North Korea during the worst of the famine. Some NGOs, perhaps correctly, argued that it was impossible to get an accurate picture of the food shortages from within the DPRK, and that interviews with the North Korean refugees in the Chinese border areas were essential to gauging the true extent of the crisis in North Korea. Such activities, however, were an embarrassment to North Korea, which quickly came to view those NGOs active in the area as hostile to the regime. Likewise, NGO representatives who spoke too openly and vividly of the depravation in North Korea were reprimanded and told how much embarrassment their words had caused.

External Factors

Interaction between NGO representatives and DPRK officials would have been difficult in the best of circumstances. As it was, it took place in the most difficult of circumstances. Not only was North Korea wrestling with continuing economic decline, massive food shortages, and a growing health crisis, but the regional security environment remained unstable. Submarine incidents and tensions along the DMZ between the North and South, the DPRK decision to test-fire a Taepo-dong missile over Japan in August 1998, lingering suspicions over North Korea's compliance with the Agreed Framework, and a suspect underground facility added tensions to the U.S.-DPRK relationship, as if the famine alone were not enough.

Cooperation with NGOs was never a priority for the DPRK leadership. NGOs were courted when necessary and generally tolerated, but never reached the level of national priority. The DPRK appeared to view the NGO involvement as a favor to the international community and a bargaining chip to be used in its international negotiations. Even those NGOs most successful at drawing a clear distinction between themselves and the U.S. government would often see their efforts fall victim to periodic tensions in U.S.-DPRK relations.

NGO ADVOCACY AND THE EVOLUTION OF POLICY TOWARD NORTH KOREA

The closed nature of the North Korean regime and the lack of independent media confirmation regarding the extent of the flooding in the country ensured that initial DPRK requests for food assistance were greeted with skepticism in Washington, as just another ploy by Pyongyang to extract resources and extort the international community. This skepticism was particularly pronounced in the U.S. intelligence community, which argued that problems in North Korea's agriculture were endemic and could not have been caused by the floods. The satellite-reliant imagery analysts also quickly concluded that the DPRK was exaggerating the extent of the flooding and the resulting damage to crops. North Korean "propaganda" was not to be believed—whether positive or negative. In hindsight, it may have been true that North Korea exaggerated the extent of the flooding to hide the systemic failures of its national economic and agriculture systems. But there is now little dispute that, whatever the cause, a famine was stalking North Korea and would soon claim thousands, if not millions, of lives. Faced with initial skepticism about an emerging famine, the international aid community and NGOs were required to make a case for action to the U.S. government, the South Korean government, and even the DPRK government itself.

Even very late into the famine, there was considerable academic doubt and disagreement about the depth and even the existence of a serious food shortage in North Korea. The firsthand reports of the NGO representatives who had visited North Korea became an important source of information. It became clear that if a response to the developing tragedy in North Korea were to be mounted, it would require a coordinated public media campaign to raise awareness of the situation. This circumstance led to a major media campaign in 1996 by an NGO consortium called Committee to Stop Famine. In addition, for a brief period, these NGOs became the first advocates to lobby on behalf of North Korea to gain political support for food assistance. As the PVOC got up and running in North Korea, the policy community and others who analyzed political developments in the country turned to NGO representatives who had visited North Korea for authoritative and on-the-ground perspectives on the severity of the North Korean food crisis. U.S. NGO efforts were ultimately compromised by the politicization of food aid and links with ongoing U.S.-DPRK negotiations. In the minds of the North Korean government, PVOC-administered food aid monitored as part of FFW projects in North Korea was from the U.S. government (distributed through the WFP in the first three cases, and then directly through the PVOC in the final case). This was "bilateral" food aid promised and delivered by the U.S. government. Thus, there was no space for an independent NGO role apart from the U.S. government, either in practice or in the minds of North Korean interlocutors.

BEYOND FOOD AID: CHALLENGES AND PROSPECTS FOR MOVING FROM RELIEF AID TO DEVELOPMENT

As North Korea has entered into what is now the seventh year since it declared itself in need of emergency humanitarian assistance as a result of flooding, it is increasingly difficult to justify North Korea's chronic food shortages as an "emergency." Even the DPRK has lessened or altogether dropped its efforts to portray its ongoing food deficit as being the result of specific natural disasters. There is also a growing sense of "donor fatigue" toward a nation that is entering its seventh consecutive year of receiving international food aid but has yet to enact any fundamental reforms in its agricultural system or economy.[21]

From the very beginning, one strategy of some U.S. NGOs has been to use food aid as a point of entry from which they might explore possible development projects through which agricultural system reforms might be introduced. According to AFSC representative Randall Ireson, "[A]s NGOs and as others who are concerned with improving the dietary and living standard in the DPRK, we should be moving as rapidly as possible beyond subsidies and toward support for change and development of the agricultural sector."[22]

Despite some easing of tensions over the past five years, engagement with North Korea still remains a political and legal minefield. While the provision of humanitarian assistance is possible, the fact that North Korea is still on the U.S. government list of State Sponsors of Terrorism, as well as still being subject to some legal strictures under the Trading with the Enemy Act, provides strict limits that complicate the challenge of moving beyond food aid to development assistance.

Another factor that cannot be ignored is an increasing dramatic downturn in the atmosphere of at least official U.S.-DPRK relations. The current Bush administration has been patently less eager to engage the DPRK, a charter member of the "Axis of Evil." In recent months, the twists and turns of official U.S.-DPRK relations have influenced even the most apolitical of the U.S. NGOs working in North Korea.

NGOS AS A SOURCE OF UNDERSTANDING ABOUT NORTH KOREA'S INTERNAL SITUATION

In the end, despite playing a niche role in addressing the immediate food crisis of the late 1990s in North Korea, the experience of U.S. NGOs in particular did not add significantly to the body of knowledge or understanding about the DPRK. This is not necessarily a criticism of the role of NGOs, but a recognition that any expectations one might have had about the degree to which NGOs have opened our window on North Korea were misplaced. Most monitors focused so intensely on fighting with the FDRC over bureaucratic details—such as the schedule and locations for monitoring visits—and were so isolated from the rest of the population that they hardly had an opportunity to learn about how North Korea actually worked. Andrew Natsios aptly expresses the challenge to NGOs of drawing accurate information about North Korea from their limited experience:

[I]n a country of 23 million people living in an area the size of Mississippi, how accurate an impression could 100 expatriate humanitarian aid workers expect to obtain? These workers, myself included, could not speak Korean, had no intimate economic or geographical knowledge of the country, and were taken on carefully supervised field trips where the citizens being visited were told ahead of time when to expect them. They were accompanied by carefully chosen government translators and transported along routes determined by central government authorities under a totalitarian political system with nearly complete control over the population. No humanitarian aid worker had ever worked in a country whose population had lived under 50 years of Orwellian control of every aspect of their lives, overseen by a secret police apparatus nearly unmatched in its pervasive control. It is not surprising that the aid workers were confused by what they saw.[23]

While NGO representatives may have had unprecedented access to North Korea, their experience has not proved to be an adequate source of understanding about North Korea. U.S. NGOs often pride themselves on their independence from the U.S. government, and many go to great lengths to establish and guard their reputations for independence. The ability of humanitarian NGOs in particular to work in some areas often relies upon their reputation for disinterest in, if not disdain for, taking sides in the political battles of the day and their focus on relieving human suffering. NGO representatives are often wary of compromising their ability to continue their work by asking too many questions or inquiring beyond the immediate scope of their particular projects. This is particularly true if it becomes clear that such inquiries will be greeted with suspicion, if not hostility. There is an even more understandable reluctance to address such sensitive issues in a public forum, particularly if an NGO has ongoing efforts in the country in question.

In addition to the questions about the inclination of NGOs to comprehend and convey a broader picture of political and economic development in North Korea, one must also question their capacity to function in this role. The North Korean resistance to aid workers with Korean language abilities and the general unfamiliarity of U.S. NGOs with North Korea meant that these NGOs were ill prepared to observe or assess broader developments in the country in which they were working.

The clearest and perhaps the most important lesson learned about North Korea through the experience of NGOs in that country is the lengths to which the DPRK regime will go to try to keep foreigners from perceiving the reality, and the priority the government places on shielding that reality from the view of the outside world. The DPRK remains sufficiently well organized and wields sufficient political control to continue such a task. More than a decade after experts predicted the imminent collapse of the regime, the DPRK government remains in control. It has been more than a decade since the collapse of the Soviet Union and eight years since the death of Kim Il Sung, yet the DPRK goes on. Despite more than seven years of continuing food shortages and an unprecedented level of opening to the international humanitarian aid community, North Korea remains apparently unshaken—perhaps largely the result of its success in controlling foreigners' access to the majority of its populace.

In early 1994, the conservative South Korean Naewoe Press published a book about the DPRK entitled *North Korea: The Land that Never Changes*. Nearly ten years later, the DPRK is hardly recognizable in comparison with its former self. In the early 1990s, no one would have dared to predict that the DPRK would admit to anything less than success in its society, let alone appeal to the international community for assistance. The notion that international aid workers and NGO monitors would be allowed to visit remote corners of North Korea was almost inconceivable. An unprecedented number of aid workers and officials have visited North Korea and engaged its citizens. One might be excused for thinking that North Korea is now more open for the interaction. While we clearly know much more today than we did a decade ago, what is more striking is how little we still know.

NOTES

1. While *juche* is most often translated into English as "self-reliance," this translation does not capture the full essence of the North Korean national ideology. *Juche* is probably best understood as a repudiation of the historical Korean mindset of *"sadaejuui"* or "respecting the great." While *juche* has gradually evolved into a nearly all-encompassing national ideology, the core concept remains that North Korea is to be the actor, not the acted upon. Thus, it is fine for the DPRK to accept assistance—as it did from China and the Soviet Union for many years—as long as North Korea is calling the shots, the master of its own destiny.

2. In the summer of 1995, North Korea requested and received 500,000 and 1.5 million metric tons in grain aid from South Korea and Japan, respectively.

3. For an excellent treatment of this economic decline, see Marcus Noland, *Avoiding the Apocalypse: The Future of the Two Koreas* (Washington, D.C.: Institute for International Economics, June 2000).

4. See Lee Hy-Sang, *North Korea: A Strange Socialist Fortress* (Westport, Conn.: Praeger, 2001), p. 192.

5. For example, this chart does not cover the activities of organizations such as the Eugene Bell Centennial Foundation (EBCF), which—while an early leader in providing food assistance to the DPRK—is also incorporated in South Korea and raised much of its aid in South Korea. Furthermore, the role of U.S. NGOs in conveying and monitoring U.S. government food aid is not reflected here. Finally, this chart relies on figures collected by the WFP and thus does not include independent contributions by religious NGOs that have not been reported publicly.

6. This number is controversial, as it includes U.S. government food aid conveyed "through" select U.S. NGOs.

7. Following the floods of August 1995, the DPRK gave annual play to localized droughts, floods, and tidal surges in what became an almost ritualized effort by the

government to save face by blaming the ongoing food shortages on a continuing stream of natural disasters beyond the regime's control.

8. See Jasper Becker, *Hungry Ghosts: Mao's Secret Famine* (New York: Free Press, 1996).

9. Another factor was the demographic distribution of the North Korean population. In contrast to South Korea and most other nations in the Asia Pacific region, the population of North Korea is distributed throughout the country remarkably evenly, with very few major urban population centers. The official explanation for this is the regime's aversion to large cities as targets for U.S. bombing. However, such distribution is also widely considered to be a control mechanism.

10. Andrew S. Natsios, *The Great North Korean Famine: Famine Politics and Foreign Policy* (Washington, D.C.: U.S. Institute of Peace Press, 2001), p. 31.

11. In this case, bilateral did not mean directly government-to-government, but rather U.S. government assistance routed through a management mechanism—the PVOC—instead of through an international organization such as the WFP.

12. Senator Frank Murkowski (R-Ark.) put it more bluntly, calling the agreement a "bribe to the North Koreans." See http://murkowski.senate.gov/releases/3-16-99-2.html.

13. U.S. General Accounting Office, U.S. Bilateral Food Assistance to North Korea Has Mixed Results, report to the Chairman and Ranking Minority Member, House Committee on International Relations, June 2000. GAO/NSIAD-00-175, 7.

14. Thomas McCarthy, "CARE's Withdrawal from North Korea," Nautilus Policy Forum Online (#00-03), 26 April 2000, www.nautilus.org.

15. http://www.careusa.org/newsroom/pressreleases/2000/apr/northkorea0404.asp.

16. This effort has been headed primarily by ADRA Switzerland.

17. For more details, see http://www.nautilus.org/dprkrenew/index.html.

18. See Park Kyung-ae, The Pattern of North Korea's Track-Two Foreign Contacts, North Pacific Policy Papers 5, Program on Canada-Asia Policy Studies, Institute of Asian Research, University of British Columbia, 2000.

19. Giorgio Maragliano, "DPRK Current Status and Prospects. Six Years of Aid: A Balance and a Possible Way Forward" (paper presented at the Fourth International Symposium on Korea and the Search for Peace in Northeast Asia, Kyoto, Japan, 17–19 November 2001). Mr. Maragliano is the ECHO representative to the DPRK.

20. Kathi Zellweger, "The Continuing Need for Food Aid and General Assistance" (presentation at the Third International NGO Conference on Humanitarian Assistance to North Korea: Cooperative Efforts Beyond Food Aid, Seoul, South Korea, 17–20 June 2001).

21. The July 2002 announcement of some early price reforms and the September 2002 announcement of a Special Administrative Region around the city of Shinuiju, on the Chinese border, are both positive developments that bear watching, but which are unlikely in the short term to have a major impact on donor attitudes toward North Korea.

22. Randall Ireson, "Agricultural Rehabilitation and Development in the DPRK: Roles for Nongovernmental Organizations" (presentation at the Third International NGO Conference on Humanitarian Assistance to North Korea: Cooperative Efforts Beyond Food Aid, Seoul, South Korea, 17-20 June 2001).

23. The Great North Korean Famine, p. 40.

Chapter Three
The European NGO Experience in North Korea

Michael Schloms

This chapter brings together the experience of the European nongovernmental organizations (NGOs) that have provided assistance to North Korea. Although NGOs are the primary sources for the following analysis, also included is the experience of international organizations in the Democratic People's Republic of Korea (DPRK), mainly United Nations (UN) agencies. Information provided by the International Federation of Red Cross and Red Crescent Societies (IFRC) is also evaluated in this chapter.

During the past six years, international aid agencies in North Korea have had to face an environment that differs significantly in numerous aspects from what they have previously experienced in humanitarian missions in other countries. Working and living conditions, negotiation practices, and restrictions on freedom of movement often lead to frustrating experiences for international aid workers. Lack of information and limited access to data are major characteristics of humanitarian action in the DPRK. The experiences of European NGOs do, however, give some insight into a country whose ideological backbone is autarky and self-reliance (*juche*), and that has nevertheless been receiving the largest amount of food aid in the history of the UN, which has been acting in response to the DPRK's aid appeal in 1995.

In 1995, Médecins Sans Frontières (MSF) was the first European NGO to begin working in North Korea. Handicap International (HI) is the latest European NGO to establish an office in Pyongyang; its program began in March 2001. Within this period of time, working conditions for NGOs in North Korea have improved modestly. The most important change, however, concerns the type of activity carried out by European NGOs. In the beginning, aid agencies mainly focused on food aid, the delivery of other aid items (such as medicine and clothes), and emergency famine relief. Today, the bulk of European NGO work—mainly funded by the European Commission (EC)—is rehabilitation of the country's agricultural system.

The reason for this shift is simple: Immediate famine relief turned out to be impossible in North Korea. Programs that by their nature required direct contact between aid workers and individual beneficiaries clashed with cultural, historical, and political realities in North Korea. Organizations such as MSF, Médecins du Monde (MDM), and Action Contre La Faim (ACF) are accustomed to implementing programs in famine-stricken countries all over the world. Out of respect for their operating principles (and due to frustrations in working with the DPRK government), these NGOs decided to withdraw.

Because of the lack of accountability, European NGOs decided to leave the bulk of food aid to UN agencies. Instead of medical emergency relief, rehabilitation of health institutions and, above all, agriculture appears to be more welcomed by North Korean authorities. Working conditions for NGOs active in these sectors are more or less the same as those for medical relief organizations, but an agronomist necessarily has differing standards than a medical doctor in terms of direct communication with individual beneficiaries or knowledge about the nutritional status of a target group. Moreover, North Korean authorities showed far more interest in mid-term agricultural recovery than in short-term famine relief.

The DPRK government's method of handling European NGOs reveals that exclusive priority is attached to the increase of domestic food production. In accordance with the country's ideological guidelines, international aid seems to be regarded as a necessary—and temporary—evil that should provide a transition to a state of food security and self-reliance, a state never achieved in the DPRK even in the best of times.

There is no reason to assume that the DRPK government's position of seeking production increases on one side and a permanent food deficit compensated by international food aid on the other will fundamentally change in the near future. Therefore, the experience of European NGOs teaches us two things. First, the restrictions on working conditions for international aid workers are unlikely to change fundamentally in the years to come, which means that the humanitarian impact of international aid cannot be accurately measured. Second, another *raison d'être* of international aid, beyond its intended humanitarian effect, has to be taken into account; namely, its beneficial impact on the skewed reality in which North Koreans have lived for more than five decades. Through their presence and their work, NGOs provide a counter-example to the worldview still propagated in North Korea. In this sense, the question of what type of aid is undertaken (relief, rehabilitation, or development) is secondary.

INITIAL ENTRY INTO NORTH KOREA: TERMS, CONDITIONS, AND OBSTACLES

Actors

Numerous European NGOs have been involved with humanitarian efforts in North Korea. As of October 2002, eight European NGOs had resident status in the DPRK and one NGO was providing aid without having a permanent residence in the country. Five other NGOs that had worked in North Korea in the past had decided to withdraw.

NGO activities began as a result of an appeal for international assistance launched by the DPRK government in 1995 after massive flooding. The first aid agency working in the DPRK was MSF, which conducted a health assistance program from November 1995 to January 1996. In general, during the first phase of their engagement, European aid agencies sent food and nonfood items (medicine, clothes, etc.) via the UN World Food Program (WFP) or the IFRC. In most cases, the delivery of aid was a response to the DPRK government's general appeal for assistance. However, some aid agencies, such as Oxfam and MSF, were directly contacted by the North Korean government through official representatives in European capitals.

In 1997, nine NGOs received residency status in the DPRK: Campus for Christus (CfC, Switzerland); Children's Aid Direct (CAD, UK); Concern Worldwide (Ireland); Cooperazione e Sviluppo (CESVI, Italy); MDM (France); MSF (French, Dutch, and Belgian sections); and German Agro Action (GAA, Germany). Oxfam Great Britain (Oxfam GB) and ACF (France) opened offices in Pyongyang in 1998, and Adventist Development and Relief Agency International (ADRA, Switzerland) and PMU InterLife (development-aid branch of the Swedish Pentecostal Mission, Sweden) followed in 1999. MDM and MSF left the country in 1998; Oxfam ended its program in 1999; ACF decided to withdraw in 2000, and CAD and Cap Anamur (German Emergency Doctors) closed their missions in 2002. Triangle-Génération Humanitaire (France) and HI (Belgian section) opened their offices in 2000 and 2001, respectively. The only European NGO based in a former socialist country is Hungarian Baptist Aid (HBAid). HBAid is currently negotiating residency status.

The majority of North Korean aid projects undertaken by European NGOs are supported by the European Commission's Humanitarian Aid Office (ECHO) and by public funds from individual European governments. Cap Anamur and CfC are financed solely by private donations.

The EC has insisted that significant levels of funding will be provided only to NGOs with residency status. In addition, it is widely assumed by observers, as well as practitioners on the ground, that the DPRK government tries to use the engagement of European countries as a counterweight to other countries considered "hostile," such as the United States, the Republic of Korea, and Japan. As a consequence, European NGOs are the only organizations (besides UN agencies) that have been permitted to set up permanent offices in Pyongyang. Having residency status in North Korea, however, does not necessarily mean improved ability to monitor projects or better insight into North Korean society. Some agencies decide to have their projects monitored by the UN Food Aid Liaison Unit (FALU) and/or the WFP and then regularly conduct their own periodic visits from outside the country, rather than relying on a highly expensive permanent office in Pyongyang run by a handful of expatriates.

From 1996 through 1998, European NGOs were active in a variety of sectors. Food delivery and food security programs aiming to improve the nutritional status of beneficiaries in the short- and mid-term were carried out by most NGOs. In the course of their engagement, agencies also focused on other fields of activity. For example, some focused on agricultural rehabilitation programs or the rehabilitation of health institutions. Oxfam GB was active in the water/sanitation sector. MSF, MDM, and ACF carried out programs of medical and nutritional emergency relief.

Most of the programs were located in the west and southwest of the DPRK (Pyongyang, South Hwanghae, North Hwanghae, South Pyongan, North Pyongan, Nampo, and Kaesong). Relatively few agencies (MSF, MDM, ACF) were present in the eastern and northeastern provinces of North and South Hamgyong.

The European aid agencies undertaking programs in the DPRK have included very different organizations. These differences are seen in organizational structure, experience, philosophical background, and specific field of activity. Contrary to U.S., South Korean, and Japanese organizations, European agencies include a type of organization often described as the "second generation" of humanitarianism. In contrast to the Red Cross movement, with its classical understanding of humanitarianism, the "French doctors" (MSF is the prototype; others are MDM and ACF) follow an approach that combines medical emergency relief and political consciousness. This "sans-frontierisme" is essentially based on nonrespect for the sovereignty of states whenever sovereignty clashes with humanitarian concerns. Furthermore, this lack of respect for sovereignty shapes the French medical agencies' understanding of neutrality and belief in the importance of bearing witness. Alain Destexhe, former secretary general of MSF International, summarizes the lesson learned in the Biafra War (1967–70) in Nigeria that led to the founding of MSF: "Humanitarianism—contrary to what the founders of the Red Cross had in mind—cannot be neutral."[1] Rony Brauman, former president of MSF France, adds: "Acting and speaking up, treating, and witnessing were the leading thoughts at the origin of MSF."[2]

It is precisely this new and wider understanding of humanitarian assistance for which MSF was awarded the Nobel Peace Prize in 1999. The Nobel Committee elaborates:

A characteristic feature of Médecins Sans Frontières is that, more clearly than anyone else, they combine...humanitarian work and work for human rights. They achieve this by insisting on their right to arouse public opinion and to point to the causes of the man-made catastrophes, namely systemic breaches of the most fundamental rights. The award to Médecins Sans Frontières is first and foremost a humanitarian award...but it is also a human rights award. [3]

Given that MSF was the prototype of the group of French medical agencies, it is hardly surprising that MSF's understanding of human rights work as a humanitarian task sharply collided with the North Korean concept of sovereignty and *juche*.

Working Conditions

According to the program manager of one European NGO, there is nothing more to say about aid agencies' maneuverability in North Korea than that it is nonexistent. He suggested that a more promising endeavor would be to conduct a study on humanitarian action in Burma. Nevertheless, it is useful to elaborate on the working conditions of European NGOs during the initial phase of their engagement in North Korea. Later, this chapter will analyze the working conditions currently faced by NGOs and discuss whether there has been any significant improvement.

The majority of aid agencies followed the requests of the North Korean authorities concerning the geographical location of their projects. In these cases, an NGO delegation was able to visit the institutions (including cooperative farms, nurseries, kindergartens, and hospitals) designated as the beneficiaries of the projects. As noted above, most projects were located in the agricultural western and southwestern provinces.

Medical relief organizations such as MSF, MDM, and ACF followed a different approach. They tried to locate their programs in those regions of the country where the humanitarian situation was reported to be particularly difficult; namely, the provinces along the east coast and in the north. Unable to conduct their own independent assessment studies, these organizations based their analyses on the findings of other observers and organizations. UN agencies described the difficult situation of these provinces in their reports. In 1999, for instance, the UN Food and Agriculture Organization (FAO) and the WFP assessment mission stated:

Some population groups, such as families receiving international food assistance and/or agricultural support, are in a better position to cope with food shortages than people in mountainous areas and in families of industrial workers, especially in non-agricultural areas....In view of these differences, the Mission expresses serious concern for the nutritional well-being of the population in areas in the Northeast of the country, which are industrial and have limited agriculture.[4]

Establishing projects in the northeast was a critical issue in the negotiations of these medical relief agencies with North Korean authorities. MDM, for example, was able to work in the eastern province of South Hamgyong only after agreeing also to establish a project in Nampo City in the west. With regard to resident

NGOs, MSF, MDM, and ACF were the only agencies in the initial phase of NGO involvement in the DPRK working in the eastern provinces of North and South Hamgyong and Kangwon.

None of the European NGOs were able to undertake preimplementation assessments that would have allowed them to design programs independently. Instead, the practice for project formulation was that the DPRK government specified beneficiary institutions and locations to the implementing organization. In most cases, the government did not grant the NGO requests to provide complete lists of institutions by geographic area. Thus, agencies were not able to estimate the impact of their aid in relation to the entire population in a specific area. This combination of lack of data and the resulting impaired understanding was perceived as one of the major obstacles to NGO work in North Korea. The four main hindrances NGOs have cited to their work in the DPRK are detailed in the following paragraphs.

First, NGO staff were confronted with considerable constraints on movement. Movement within Pyongyang city was restricted; even driving a car without a driver was usually prohibited. Outside Pyongyang, restrictions were even tighter. NGO expatriate staff members were not allowed to leave their hotels or move within a specified zone without a North Korean staff member escorting them. A number of cases, however, demonstrate that even the harshest restrictions cannot totally inhibit international aid workers from stealing a glance behind the curtain. Some of these experiences will be presented in the next section.

Second, all international agencies, including UN agencies, had access only to specified DPRK counties. In May 1997, for instance, 159 out of 211 counties were accessible. The remaining counties were off-limits; according to the government, this was due to national security concerns. All aid agencies agreed that no aid programs or humanitarian distributions were to be carried out in nonaccessible areas.

Third, in areas where there has been access, constraints on movement have remained. Not all counties declared generally accessible by North Korean authorities were accessible to all NGOs. For example, when an agency requested access to a county where another agency was working, access was often denied. Within areas where an NGO had established projects, considerable restrictions on program monitoring had to be accepted. Aid agencies were required to inform the Flood Damage Rehabilitation Committee (FDRC) one week in advance which institutions they planned to visit. Sometimes the proposal was rejected; in some cases, the rejection came shortly before the requested date of the visit. In most cases, however, the travel plans were accepted by the FDRC. In the first years of NGO engagement in North Korea, the situation presented to European NGOs on their visits sometimes seemed to be worse than expected. In other cases, by contrast, institution staff appeared to make an effort to highlight progress and improvements.

Fourth, on monitoring visits, NGO staff were accompanied by local authorities and representatives from the FDRC (including a translator, since one of the provisions for being able to work in the DPRK was minimal or no Korean language ability). Within institutions, the stock (food, medicine, heating material, etc.) could be checked. Visiting infirmaries in hospitals, however, was sometimes problematic. Communication with individuals during monitoring visits was only possible via an interpreter assigned by the FDRC. Some NGOs report that they often had the impression that the interpreter filtered the questions and/or answers; sometimes it seemed that patients' answers were prearranged.

In sum, during their monitoring visits, NGOs were able to check whether distributed items reached the designated institutions. Aid agencies unanimously report that food, medicine, clothing, heating material, and other items reached the institutions. The end use of these supplies, however, could not be monitored by NGO staff.

In the first years of European NGO engagement in North Korea, food aid was an important project focus. Most of these agencies had extensive experience with humanitarian crises and famines in other parts of the world. The challenge in other countries had often been the organization of food aid in environments characterized by a lack of governmental and administrative structures. In North Korea, however, NGOs found an entirely different situation. In a sense, the DPRK was the exact opposite of a failed state. Particularly when it came to the issue of food and food distribution, the state was, and still is, omnipresent. For decades, the distribution of food has been the task of the government, which has established a highly complex and bureaucratic Public Distribution System (PDS). Since the DPRK is a highly industrialized country, only about one-third of the population works in the agricultural sector.[5] The remaining population receives food rations, via the PDS, in the distribution center of a district or institution.

Newly arrived European NGOs' perception of the PDS varied greatly. Some regarded it as a reliable and highly efficient mechanism that guaranteed an equitable distribution of resources. For others, the PDS was a political tool with which the government kept the population under control. In their view, PDS rations differed considerably according to a wide range of criteria, including political loyalty to the government. It is noteworthy that neither faction was in a position to base its view on reliable data or concrete observations.

All food aid allocated by European NGOs—resident and nonresident—was distributed via the PDS. If an agency targeted a particular group of people (children, pregnant women, elderly people, etc.), the items were distributed to designated institutions via either PDS centers within the institutions or the district's distribution centers. If an organization wanted to cover a geographical area without specifying a certain group of beneficiaries, the food was distributed via the PDS structures in the district concerned. Distributing food outside the PDS, as requested by agencies with a critical view of the PDS, was not allowed by the authorities.

International staff were able to check whether the aid items reached the PDS. However, whether the PDS effectively focused the distribution of these items to designated target groups could not be monitored. UN agencies and most of the

NGOs engaged in food aid were convinced that the PDS did effectively target the selected groups. Some irregularities were regarded as exceptions caused by a lack of training and understanding of local staff rather than proof of systemic abuse of aid. For example, in 1997, it appeared that a consignment of high-energy milk contributed by CAD and designated for therapeutic feeding of children in institutions had been used for general distribution. However, according to CAD, this was due to a lack of understanding by institution staff.[6]

NGOs unanimously report that the number of expatriate, permanent staff has been one of the thorniest issues in their negotiations with the FDRC. As a result, NGOs have been able to get only a very limited number of expatriates into North Korea—on average, not more than four per agency. In terms of expatriate staff, MSF was the biggest NGO, with 13 aid workers. No Korean-speaking international staff have been permitted to enter the country as expatriate, permanent aid workers.

"North Korea is our only mission without local staff" is a statement often heard from NGO representatives. The national staff members are perceived as "minders," rather than local staff. The national staff are paid by the agency but assigned by the FDRC. Some NGOs complain that the national staff are changed rather frequently, which is not conducive to effective work. Agencies have had no influence on the employment or discharge of their national staff.

In short, aid agencies have not had a sufficient number of staff in relation to the size of their projects. In Guatemala, for instance, MSF supports three health and children's institutions with seven expatriates. In North Korea, ACF supported 2,400 institutions with nine expatriate aid workers.

Finally, communication among NGOs has been hindered in several ways. Joint monitoring visits, for instance, are not permitted. As noted above, a county that has one agency present is often not accessible to others. In addition, aid agencies have not been allowed to equip themselves with any form of mobile communications equipment.

THE DECISION TO LEAVE: MDM, MSF, ACF, AND OXFAM

The Experience of Medical Relief Organizations

MDM was the first NGO to withdraw from North Korea. The organization made its decision in July 1998, after having worked in the country for about 10 months. MSF, which began implementing programs in the DPRK in January 1997, made the same decision in September 1998. ACF, which started its programs in January 1998, pulled out in spring 2000. These three organizations were the only NGOs in the DPRK focusing on emergency medical and nutritional programs, that is, short-term famine relief projects consisting of food and medical assistance.

MDM was founded in France in 1980 by a group of relief workers who had formerly worked for MSF. Bernard Kouchner, MDM's first president, was also one of the founders of MSF. Since its founding, MDM has become one of the largest humanitarian NGOs in France, with delegations and offices in 16 countries.

Beginning in fall 1997, the French section of MDM carried out a nutritional and medical program in South Hamgyong. The program had three components: therapeutic centers established in hospitals and children's institutions; health structures supported by donation of medicines and training of medical staff; and a surgical-support program, established in a hospital in South Hamgyong. In addition, high-energy milk was distributed to children's institutions.

MSF, founded in France in 1971 and now one of the biggest international humanitarian NGOs, provides medical assistance to populations in more than 80 countries. MSF started work in North Korea in 1995. Medical and nutritional relief programs were implemented from July 1997 to September 1998 in South Pyongan, Kangwon, and North Hwanghae. In February 1998, the project was extended to the province of North Hamgyong. The nutritional program was designed to target severely malnourished children and consisted of feeding centers in the pediatric wards of county and provincial hospitals. Training was organized for the staff of these wards and materials were distributed to the institutions. Expatriate human resources and budget issues were divided among various sections of MSF. MSF-Belgium was in charge of South Pyongan and North Hamgyong, MSF-Netherlands covered North Hwanghae, and MSF-France covered activities in Kangwon province.

ACF was founded in France in 1979 and specializes in nutrition, food security, health, and water treatment. Today, ACF has sections in Spain, the UK, and the United States. From January 1998 to spring 2000, ACF carried out a nutritional program designed to support nurseries in the province of North Hamgyong. This program also included activities in pediatric hospitals and the training of staff in nurseries and kindergartens.

In sum, the field of activity of these relief organizations in the DPRK was very similar. The very nature of the types of programs they ran requires that aid workers get in direct contact with the population. As one MDM nutritionist notes:

Our aim was to bring assistance—in direct contact with the people—to a population in an emergency situation. However, we were deprived of the liberty of movement, of the liberty to communicate, and of the right to care for our patients. We had no access to the people and no access to information that would have allowed us to evaluate our programs.[7]

Beyond direct contact with patients, medical relief organizations regarded it as necessary to include in their projects training programs for local medical staff. It quickly became evident to international medical staff that their North Korean counterparts had had little or no interaction with international colleagues during the past few decades. Consequently, their skills reflected the standard of knowledge of the 1960s and 1970s. International staff saw a lack of knowledge in terms of the treatment of malnutrition, modern surgery methods, and the use of modern medical drugs. The use of antibiotics, in particular, revealed that doctors were not familiar with indications, contraindications, and the creation of resistance. Thus, the delivery of medical equipment and drugs was combined with training sessions.

According to an MDM official, the organization had experienced constraints in freedom of movement in numerous missions in several countries. In these other missions, however, MDM knew that the relief activities were not in vain. In North Korea, MDM did not have this certainty and doubted the beneficial impact of its programs. Therefore, MDM decided to pull out, even though the organization had no doubt that the humanitarian situation in North Korea was serious. According to MDM's president, "[H]aving to end a mission means to abandon people who are certainly in great need."[8] MDM did not criticize the remaining agencies for continuing their work. On the contrary, with its decision to withdraw, MDM wanted to exert pressure on the DPRK government that would improve working conditions for those NGOs remaining in the country. MDM's decision to withdraw did not have negative repercussions on the environment for NGOs in North Korea and was widely respected by the remaining aid agencies.

During the course of its engagement in North Korea, the MSF sections came to the conclusion that their nutritional programs did not reach the target group of severely malnourished children under the age of five. MSF's findings were, first, that—contrary to official statements by the FDRC—the program did not cover all institutions in the given geographic areas. Second, large numbers of acutely malnourished children living in the target region did not frequent the institutions supported by MSF.

At the beginning of the program, the FDRC gave MSF a list of all health facilities in each county in the catchment area. During field trips, however, the MSF team saw institutions that were not mentioned on these lists. Furthermore, MSF questioned the population figures given by the FDRC. When asked for a more complete list, the provincial authorities told MSF that data could be distributed only by the central government.

During the course of the program, roughly 14,000 children were treated in 64 feeding centers. MSF estimated that this figure represented less than 1 percent of the target group (children under five in the designated geographic areas). Furthermore, MSF observed that vulnerable groups of children had no access to the institutions supported by MSF. On one of their field trips, the Belgian section of MSF saw a building with children who were evidently in very poor physical condition. After negotiations with local authorities, MSF was allowed to visit this building. The children were in a state of health much worse than those children MSF had seen in institutions covered by its aid program. The physical, psychological, and hygienic state of these children led MSF to the conclusion that they must have lived in the streets for a period of time.[9]

Convinced that their aid was not reaching the groups of the population in greatest need, MSF tried to renegotiate the scope of its activities. The government, however, asked MSF instead to deliver pharmaceutical raw materials rather than set up nutritional programs. In September 1998, MSF decided to withdraw from North Korea. Contrary to MDM months before, MSF publicly criticized the government and those aid agencies that preferred to continue their work. Thus, MSF's withdrawal had a very negative impact on the environment for the remaining NGOs and their relationship with the government.[10]

During the course of its programs and field visits, ACF came to conclusions very similar to those of MSF. In 450 monitoring visits to nurseries and kindergartens in North Hamgyong, ACF discovered that only 45 percent of the registered children were actually present in the institutions. Moreover, of the total number of children being treated in the feeding centers set up by ACF, only 1 percent were chronically malnourished and 0.1 percent acutely malnourished. According to the general assumption that the population of North Hamgyong had been particularly hard-hit by the famine (as confirmed by the joint EU/WFP/UNICEF study[11]), the actual percentage of malnourished children in this province was believed by ACF to be much higher. In fact, ACF staff saw malnourished children in the streets of the provincial capital of Chungjin. In view of these findings and observations, ACF wanted to establish street kitchens in the province of North Hamgyong so as to better target vulnerable population groups. This proposal was denied by the North Korean authorities. Thus, ACF decided to leave the country in March 2000. ACF did not publicly criticize the aid agencies that remained in the DPRK.

MDM, MSF, and ACF were taking part in the coordinating mechanisms established by UN agencies for resident NGOs (sector meetings) and by ECHO (regular meetings of all ECHO-funded NGOs). In statements issued after their decisions to withdraw, these medical relief organizations stressed the need for a common and firm position for aid agencies with regard to humanitarian principles and for respect for international standards in North Korea. As a reaction to the withdrawal of MDM and MSF, the remaining agencies formed a Common Humanitarian Action Plan in November 1998 that included a set of fundamental principles, including access for assessment, monitoring, and evaluation. It was widely understood by the signing agencies that these principles had to be regarded as objectives in the DPRK.

The Experience of Oxfam and Cap Anamur

Medical relief work requires working conditions that, according to the above-mentioned relief agencies, are not met in the DPRK. However, two NGOs that were active mainly in rehabilitation programs decided to withdraw from the country: Oxfam and Cap Anamur. Their experience shall be briefly presented here.

Oxfam, founded in 1942 in Oxford, UK, as the "Oxford Committee for Famine Relief" is one of the oldest and largest humanitarian NGOs. Originally set up to highlight humanitarian needs in Greece after the country's invasion by Nazi Germany, Oxfam International is today a confederation of NGOs based in 12 countries. Oxfam has traditionally focused on public health and food security. Two sections were involved with humanitarian aid for North Korea: Oxfam Hong Kong provided food aid to the WFP and food for children to UNICEF. Oxfam GB was implementing an ECHO-funded water treatment program in

Pyongyang City, South Pyongan, and North and South Hwanghae. Oxfam GB gained residency status in 1998. The water treatment program, supervised by three to four expatriates, ended in December 1999. North Korean authorities had wanted the program to continue, but Oxfam GB decided against doing so. Oxfam Hong Kong ended its food supply program when the government did not renew its request.

The North Korean government had first contacted Oxfam GB through its representative in London, asking for aid projects in the water/sanitation sector, traditionally a very strong point for Oxfam GB. Indeed, Oxfam GB was the only NGO implementing programs in this field. The program consisted of the delivery of chlorine and the introduction of modern water treatment technology. In the beginning, Oxfam GB intended to work in the northeast of the country. The government, however, only allowed assessment activities in the southwest. Following its limited assessment studies, Oxfam GB was convinced that needs in these areas were great and agreed to work in the proposed provinces. One industrial plant that had formerly produced chlorine for the entire country had reportedly collapsed. Thus, Oxfam GB regarded the lack of chlorine treatment, combined with the nutritional status of the population, as an extreme risk.

At the beginning of its engagement, the British NGO had a long-term perspective: It hoped for a gradual geographic extension of the water treatment program to the northeast part of the country. In addition, Oxfam GB hoped that this type of program could be the starting point for a multisection engagement with the DPRK. In other words, after getting in, Oxfam GB hoped to gradually open the door. Over the course of the program, however, Oxfam GB observed that the door was slowly closing.

Oxfam GB was well aware that conducting assessment studies using international standards was not possible in North Korea. These standards would have required direct contact with consumers—household visits, direct contact with technical staff in water treatment plants, and unhindered access to hospitals in order to check for the presence of water-borne diseases. Working conditions in the DPRK, however, were worse than expected and continued to worsen. To Oxfam GB it seemed that the authorities regarded the NGO as a deliverer of chlorine and technological know-how. Therefore, chlorine stocks could be visited by Oxfam GB, but the testing of water was a more difficult issue. At no time was Oxfam GB able to conduct comprehensive water tests or gather data concerning the spread of water-borne diseases. Thus, it was impossible to measure the program's impact.

Like medical relief organizations, Oxfam GB came to the conclusion that a number of fundamental NGO principles were not respected in the DPRK. The lack of accountability and demonstrable impact led Oxfam GB to the decision not to extend its program after the planned end of the first project in December 1999. Oxfam GB agreed not to take a high profile and did not publicly criticize the North Korean government or those aid agencies remaining in the country. After its announcement to pull out, Oxfam GB was told by the FDRC that its demands would be met. The NGO, however, was convinced that this offer was a tactical statement rather than the result of a substantive shift of opinion and ultimately withdrew.

A similar decision has been taken by Cap Anamur, an NGO founded in 1975 and exclusively funded by private donations. Cap Anamur started working in North Korea in 1998 and initially focused on the rehabilitation of health institutions in South Hwanghae province. The program had been extended so that Cap Anamur supported health and children's' institutions in South Hwanghae, South Pyongan and North Hamgyong province. Activities included the rehabilitation of operating theaters, sanitation facilities, and kitchens, as well as distribution of food, drugs, clothing, and other items to health institutions.

In fall 2002, Cap Anamur reviewed its activities in North Korea and decided to take an unprecedented approach. In a "Memorandum to the DPRK government," Cap Anamur criticized the working conditions in the country as a major obstacle to effective aid work: "Under normal circumstances, we easily would have been able to achieve in 12 months what we actually achieved in DPRK in five years."[12] Thus, the NGO demanded considerable improvements concerning its operational space and at the same time declared its preparedness to provide aid on a major scale. The offer included the proposal to rehabilitate the entire health infrastructure for rural populations in two districts in the southwest of the country (an estimated aid amount of two to three million US Dollars). Inter alia, Cap Anamur demanded the independent recruitment of local staff, visits of project sites without prior notification, the establishment of sub-offices in the project area, and the permission for expatriates to drive a car outside Pyongyang. The FDRC declined these demands by stating that they are "not compatible with the rules and working principles now valid for all international and non-governmental organizations working in our country."[13]

Noteworthy, according to Cap Anamur workers, this decision was taken by the central FDRC against the will of local authorities that had established a good working relationship with the NGO.

CURRENT EUROPEAN NGO ACTIVITIES IN NORTH KOREA

Programs

The focus of European NGOs in North Korea has changed in recent years. After the withdrawal of MDM, MSF, and ACF, no nutritional or therapeutic programs have been implemented by NGOs. In addition, food aid—compared to the first years of NGO engagement in North Korea—is playing a far less important role. Resident agencies, including the IFRC, came to the conclusion that food aid should be largely left to the WFP and the FALU. The IFRC had succeeded in distributing food aid outside the PDS. The intention had been to provide food rations to vulnerable groups in addition to regular PDS rations.

However, the beneficiaries had received the IFRC rations as a substitute for rather than a supplement to the PDS rations. Therefore, the IFRC decided not to continue the food aid program.

Generally speaking, European NGOs now focus on mid-term rehabilitation projects rather than activities aiming to achieve short-term famine relief. The main fields of activity are agricultural rehabilitation and food security programs, as the following illustrates.

ADRA Switzerland was founded in 1986 as a branch of the ADRA network. ADRA Switzerland is implementing a unique program in North Hwanghae province, aiming to improve the energy supply for nurseries, kindergartens, orphanages, and hospitals. Since 1999, ADRA Switzerland has produced and installed solar mirrors and solar kitchens for these institutions. The project is currently funded by the UN Office for the Coordinator of Humanitarian Affairs (OCHA). In addition, ADRA Switzerland distributes food, clothes, and other non-food items. Two expatriates are supervising the activities.

CfC, founded in 1973, is implementing a project to improve the livelihood of about 8,000 beneficiaries—mainly farmers' families in South Hwanghae. The program aims to improve local knowledge of pastoral agriculture, forage cultivation, and goat husbandry.

CAD is a British NGO founded in 1990 that has been active in North Korea since 1996. CAD opened an office in Pyongyang in 1997, focusing on relief operations in South Pyongan province. In 1999, CAD was able to move its program to the eastern province of South Hamgyong. The project included a food security program (rehabilitation and construction of greenhouses and delivery of seeds) and a winter support program (distribution of clothing and boots to children in institutions). In addition, CAD was carrying out a rehabilitation program in the Hamhung Maternity Hospital and a water and sanitation program. CAD received funds from ECHO, the Swedish International Development Cooperation Agency (SIDA), and the NGO Funding Mechanism, which provides bridging funds for resident NGOs and is managed by OCHA. Due to financial constraints, CAD had to close its programs in 2002.

Food security and agricultural recovery is the main field of activity as well for Concern Worldwide, an Irish NGO founded in 1968. Concern has assisted cooperative farms in South Pyongan province with multiple cropping programs. Agricultural inputs (seeds, fertilizer, sprayers, etc.) and technical advice have been provided and a tree nurseries program (fuel-wood trees) has been launched. Concern established an office in North Korea in 1997 and is currently staffed with three international aid workers. It receives funds from the Irish government, SIDA, ECHO, the EC's Directorate-General for Development (EC DG/DEV), and the NGO Funding Mechanism.

CESVI, founded in Italy in 1985, started to work in the DPRK in 1997 with health projects in South Hwanghae and Kaesong provinces. Since 1999, CESVI has focused on agricultural projects in those provinces supporting double-cropping programs and livestock production. Other activities include a Food for Work

(FFW) program (repair of an embankment) and the distribution of coal and winter clothing to children's institutions and hospitals. Two expatriates are based in Pyongyang. CESVI's projects are financed by ECHO, EC DG/DEV, and the NGO Funding Mechanism.

GAA was founded in 1962 and is today one of the biggest private development organizations in Germany. Over the course of its activity in North Korea, which started in 1997, GAA shifted its focus from emergency relief to agricultural rehabilitation. Current programs aim to raise productivity of cooperative farms through agricultural inputs (seeds, fertilizer, pesticides), crop diversification, and food processing projects. In addition, GAA aims to improve food security by constructing greenhouses and supporting the local production of fortified biscuits for school children. Projects are located in South Hwanghae and North Pyongan. GAA receives funds from the German government, ECHO, and the NGO Funding Mechanism. In terms of aid amount and number of expatriate staff, GAA is currently the biggest NGO present in the DPRK. The implementation of its program is overseen by nine expatriates based in a permanent office in Pyongyang.

The most recent European NGO to start work in North Korea is HI's Belgian section. This section was founded in 1986 and launched a program in the DPRK in March 2001. According to its mandate and traditional field of activity, HI Belgium addresses the needs of disabled people in North Korea. It provides support to an orthopedic factory and an orthopedic hospital, both in Hamhung, South Hamgyong province. HI Belgium hopes to be able to widen the scope of its activities in the DPRK in the future; the organization has established a permanent office and receives funds from ECHO.

HBAid is the only European NGO working in North Korea based in a former DPRK ally state. As a nonresident NGO, HBAid delivered and distributed relief goods to orphanages and hospitals in January and February 2001. HBAid is currently negotiating residency status.

Agricultural recovery and food security programs are also run by the Swedish church-based aid agency PMU Interlife (the development aid branch of the Swedish Pentecostal Mission). Beyond agricultural inputs for cooperative farms, PMU Interlife assists schools and health care institutions with coal and other basic needs. PMU Interlife has a permanent office and is running programs in South Pyongan province funded by SIDA. The first program, located in Songchon county in South Pyongan province, was closed in June 2000 because the county was declared inaccessible by North Korean authorities. A new site was proposed and a similar project was established.

Since December 2000, Triangle-Génération Humanitaire, an NGO founded in 1994 and based in France, has established an office and is providing agricultural support. In South Pyongan, Triangle assists nine cooperative farms with agricultural inputs and soil rehabilitation. The program also includes rehabilitation of irrigation systems and environmental protection projects. Triangle receives funds from the EC DG/DEV.

Maneuverability: Progress and Stagnation

If one compares the conditions under which NGOs currently work in North Korea with the working conditions of the initial phase of NGO engagement, some improvements can be observed. In a number of respects, however, no change for the better can be detected.

As far as assessment and survey issues are concerned, European NGOs have not seen fundamental improvement. It is still the DPRK government that designates the institutions and provides beneficiary figures to NGOs. Independent preimplementation assessment studies are not allowed. Furthermore, NGOs as well as UN agencies still have no access to complete data regarding numbers and location of institutions in any given area. Crop and food supply are assessed by an FAO satellite system and joint FAO/WFP missions that visit North Korea twice a year. These assessment missions have experienced a steady improvement of working conditions and have even included household visits. Data on cereal production and food supply provided by the FAO and the WFP are the basis for UN agencies' and NGOs' appeals to international donors.

Undertaking nutrition surveys, however, remains problematic. The results of the joint UNICEF/WFP/EU nutrition survey in 1998 were widely discussed in the international media and highlighted the poor nutritional status of children. Some observers assume that this experience led the North Korean government to prohibit future nutrition surveys. Despite pressure from governmental and nongovernmental organizations, no nutrition surveys, including any by international aid agencies, have been undertaken since 1998.

With regard to the location of aid programs, however, considerable improvements have been achieved. As noted above, the majority of European NGO projects were initially located in the southwestern part of the country, following the direction of the FDRC. From the beginning of NGO involvement, however, the organizations have had the goal of extending activities to the east and north, where the population is believed to have fewer resources to cope with food shortages. In 1999, CAD was able to move from South Pyongan province in the west to South Hamgyong province in the east. GAA was permitted to expand its scope of activities to North Pyongan province in 2000. The success of CAD and GAA can be explained by two factors. First, both NGOs are mainly active in a sector accorded high priority by the North Korean authorities (agricultural rehabilitation). Second, both agencies claim to have built up a relatively good relationship with their counterparts (e.g., they do not encounter problems faced by a number of other aid agencies, such as difficulties with visa issuance).

UN agencies consider it desirable to further increase the resident NGO presence to provide greater geographic coverage. For instance, since ACF's withdrawal in spring 2000, only Cap Anamur has been working in the particularly hard hit province of North Hamgyong.

In addition, regional access has improved considerably during the past few years. As of October 2001, 167 of 211 counties are accessible to international aid agencies. According to the former UN humanitarian coordinator in the DPRK, David Morton, 75 percent of the North Korean population lives in these accessible counties. The freedom of movement for international staff within the accessible areas has improved only modestly, however. Restrictions on movement within Pyongyang have been eased somewhat; it is now possible to drive a car without a North Korean driver and to leave a hotel without an escort, for example. Field trips and monitoring visits, however, have to be announced to the FDRC in advance and, in principle, are subject to the same restrictions as in the beginning of NGO work in North Korea. Some change can be observed as far as the arrangement of visits is concerned. In recent years, NGOs have frequently reported that local staff have tended to highlight achievements and coping strategies rather than needs, weaknesses, and poor conditions.

The effects of international food aid are contested even within the UN. In February 2001, UN special rapporteur for food rights Jean Ziegler noted, "[M]ost of the international food aid was being diverted by the army, the secret services, and the government."[14] The WFP, in contrast, claims that international food aid in North Korea has "averted a famine."[15] Thus, former WFP executive director Catherine Bertini criticized Ziegler's statement as "unsubstantiated, not referenced, and...not based on first-hand observation."[16]

There is no proof for one claim or the other. International aid agencies cannot control the distribution of food aid to individual beneficiaries. They can only monitor the distribution of food to the PDS. All aid agencies report that the aid reaches the PDS stations. Whether designated population groups are effectively targeted by the PDS and what impact the food aid has had so far on the nutritional status of vulnerable groups are beyond the control of aid agencies. In an article on humanitarian action in North Korea published by ACF, Christophe Reltien said:

One of the major constraints is that all humanitarian aid must be channeled through Korea's state distribution system.... Access to the most vulnerable sectors of the population is a major objective, but one of the reasons for their vulnerability is precisely their exclusion from the system under which humanitarian aid is distributed.[17]

Asked whether it was the people in greatest need or the military and political elite who benefited from international food aid, one UN official answered, "We don't know." This seems to be the only honest answer. A comprehensive, random-based, and periodic nutritional survey would be the only means to resolve the debate, but under current restrictions this is an impossibility.

Staffing issues remain problematic in the DPRK. The total number of international staff in the country is about 110. NGOs are staffed with two to four expatriates each. UN agencies and NGOs consider their staff situation unsatisfactory in view of the extent of their commitment. Some NGOs report that they have encountered problems with visa issuance. Others, however, observed that a good relationship with the FDRC has helped to avoid these problems. In terms of communications equipment, no improvement has occurred since the initial phase of humanitarian activities in the DPRK.

In sum, considerable improvements have been made, but implementing better assessment and monitoring standards, as well as improving staffing ratios, remain on the agenda. It is noteworthy that in the view of NGOs as well as UN agencies, the positive changes are not due to improvements in the general political climate on the Korean Peninsula. For example, no agency observed any significant improvement in relations as a result of the June 2000 inter-Korean summit or the establishment of diplomatic ties between the DPRK and a number of European countries.[18] The building of trust and the development of mutual respect and understanding are given as the main reasons for the improvements achieved in a country that, before 1995, had never come in contact with terms such as "NGO" or "monitoring."

As far as UN agencies are concerned, the withholding or redirection of assistance and public criticism are not used as bargaining chips in negotiations with the North Korean side. In the event that the North Korean counterpart has not respected a settled agreement, however, UN agencies have taken the step of withholding assistance. Based on the UN's experience, it seemed that the FDRC did not respect signed agreements, particularly in terms of staffing issues.

BEYOND FOOD AID: CHALLENGES AND PROSPECTS FOR MOVING FROM RELIEF AID TO DEVELOPMENT

Prospects

The debate on linking relief, rehabilitation, and development came up in the aftermath of humanitarian missions after the end of the Cold War—particularly in the context of the Rwanda crisis where warring parties manipulated aid. In 1996, the EC postulated that in an emergency situation

[R]elief actions should, apart from their primary objective of saving the lives of victims, take account of the longer-term objectives of reconstruction and development....[R]ehabilitation actions should be undertaken so as to ensure the most effective transition from emergency assistance to long-term development.[19]

Some scholars have argued that the transition from relief to development assistance would prevent humanitarian aid from being manipulated. For example, Mary B. Anderson introduced a "do-no-harm" approach, theorizing, "[A]id workers should try to identify local capacities for peace and connectors and design their aid programs to support and reinforce them."[20]

In the North Korean context, one statement is heard consistently from donor representatives and NGOs: "We cannot give relief aid indefinitely." The second argument in favor of a move from relief to development is the need to address the root causes instead of the symptoms.[21] Increasing the production of food by providing agricultural inputs and by assisting the industrial and energy sector is regarded as being a more reasonable enterprise than giving food aid. In the water/sanitation sector as well, wells and pipes have been identified as a fundamental problem that the delivery of chlorine does not address.

The basic idea that relief aid can only be provided for a limited period of time and should lead to longer-term rehabilitation and development activities is common sense. The institutional linkage of relief, rehabilitation, and development and the postulate of embedding humanitarianism in longer-term strategies, however, have been criticized by some scholars and humanitarian organizations as being incompatible with the classical understanding of humanitarian action as a means of saving human lives. Different fields of activity coincide with differing ethical frameworks and conceptualizations of neutrality, so that a move from relief to development implies a corresponding move from one set of actors to another.[22]

In North Korea, this shift has already been made. NGOs focusing on short-term medical and nutritional relief have left the country. The remaining aid agencies, as noted above, pursue mid-term rehabilitation objectives, mainly in the agricultural sector. Other programs include the training of local medical staff or farmers. Thus, as far as the activities of European NGOs are concerned, the move from relief to rehabilitation—being the first step toward development aid—has been accomplished during the past few years.

Also, the shift from relief to rehabilitation has already been advocated and agreed upon by a number of important actors, including the DPRK government. In 1998, the United Nations Development Program (UNDP) brought together for the first time delegations from the North Korean government, donor countries, and aid agencies at "Thematic Roundtable Meetings on Agricultural Recovery and Environmental Protection (AREP) in the DPRK." Thus, a general willingness to support longer-term projects in North Korea has already been established. The DPRK approval of the AREP initiative must be noted as significant. Some observers see the government's participation in the AREP process as "evidence that North Korea is slowly accommodating international interests and presence and has implicitly recognized the structural nature of the food crisis."[23] There are no empirical data, however, that would show whether this optimistic view is true, or whether the AREP process is merely seen by the DPRK as a new means to capture additional UN and donor funds.

The European Union strongly supports the implementation of development aid in North Korea. The EC's responsible body (Europe Aid Cooperation Office) has, in principle, expressed its willingness to fund development projects in the DPRK.

Obstacles

The shift from humanitarian relief to development assistance faces three sets of problems related to North Korea's political environment, the nature of the humanitarian crisis, and the crisis's root causes.

The question of whether relief should be linked to a set of conditions is highly contested. The practice of conditioning development assistance, however, is beyond dispute. However, there are differences concerning the set of criteria that should be applied to funds for development. The political reality in North Korea clashes with most of the guidelines established by international donors. If one considers the experience of humanitarian organizations over the past six years, it seems nearly impossible for North Korea to comply with such prerequisites as the strengthening of civil society, cooperation with local (nongovernmental) actors, and the targeting of particular population groups.

Given the incompatibility of the North Korean environment with the standards of development aid, the move from relief to longer-term development aid will depend on the political will of western governments, rather than on the independent decisions of donor institutions. European countries, especially Scandinavian countries, are known to be "softer" about criteria for development aid. So far, however, even the Scandinavian countries are reluctant when it comes to North Korea. Already, rehabilitation and development programs, including AREP, are generally underfunded.[24]

The second obstacle to a move toward development assistance is related to the nature of the DPRK's ongoing humanitarian crisis. Although no reliable or complete data on the population's nutritional status are available, it is widely accepted that the emergency is not yet over. The situation in North Korea, often described as a "slow-motion famine,"[25] requires emergency aid even in the eighth year of international assistance. According to the UN's Consolidated Inter-Agency Appeal for DPRK 2001, the first objective remains to "provide food aid and a nutritional safety-net to the most vulnerable, thus averting a famine."

Therefore, it is widely agreed that development aid should complement relief aid without substituting for it, at least not in the short run. Consequently, a move toward development assistance means that donor governments have to mobilize additional resources for North Korea. Given the lack of information and accountability of aid efforts so far, the additional mobilization of funds appears problematic.

The third obstacle is the fact that rehabilitation and development programs that focus on an increase in food production are unlikely to address the root causes of the food crisis in North Korea. Under the omnipresent ideology of *juche,* North Korea was unable to respond to the loss of its socialist trading partners after 1989.[26] Imports of food, energy, and agricultural inputs drastically decreased, forcing the country's highly industrialized agriculture gradually to revert to preindustrialization cultivation methods.[27] Therefore, attempts to increase national production will still address the symptoms rather than the causes. A study on food security in North Korea concluded: "Since domestic production alone is unlikely to meet even minimum human needs, such a strategy appears quite limiting. Escape from the famine will almost surely require at least some liberalization of trade policies."[28] It remains to be seen whether development or relief aid is more likely to raise North Korea's consciousness of the need for economic policy changes.[29]

NGO AS A WINDOW ON NORTH KOREA'S INTERNAL SITUATION

The DPRK Government's Handling of the Crisis

Several communist countries in Asia have experienced food shortages and famines in the past. If one compares the North Korean crisis with the situation in Mongolia (early 1930s), North Vietnam (1955–56), mainland China (1959–61), or Cambodia (1977–79), two major differences limit the DPRK government's maneuverability.

First, in the cases mentioned above, more than 80 percent of the population worked in agriculture. North Korea, in contrast, is a highly industrialized country where less than 30 percent of the people work on state and collective farms.[30] In other Asian countries, the food shortage hit large population sectors, including the food-producing groups. Therefore, attempts to increase food production led directly to an improvement of the nutritional status of large population groups. In North Korea, food producers and those hit by the famine are two different population groups.

The second aspect relates to the ideological context. In the above cases, crisis situations were finally ended by implementing market-oriented reforms. This required a certain ideological flexibility by political leaders. In view of the dynastic character of the North Korean regime, this flexibility for a long time appeared as illusionary. Economist Marcus Noland notes:

The point is that reformers in both China and Vietnam were relatively free to construct tortured rationalizations about how market-oriented reforms were what Marx, Mao, or Ho really had in mind. The ideological terrain faced by the current North Korean regime is very different.[31]

This might explain why the North Korean government did not introduce any major economic reform during the peak of the famine in 1995-1997. As recently as in summer 2002, a number of market-oriented measures in the country's economic and financial structure have been undertaken. It remains to be seen whether these steps are the beginning of North Korea following the Chinese model, as some observers have noted.[32]

The way North Korean authorities have been dealing with European NGOs over the past six years illustrates that the government's conflict management focuses on the increase of food production. Although in principle all NGOs encounter the same set of problems in the DPRK in terms of working conditions, some differences—and thus priorities—become obvious when it comes to different areas of activities.

In their negotiations with the FDRC about the design of projects, medical relief organizations concluded that the FDRC did not attribute importance to medical assistance programs. The experience of humanitarian aid agencies during famines and their general medical knowledge, however, suggested that food aid without therapeutic care does not effectively address malnutrition.[33] The FDRC clearly emphasized agricultural rehabilitation programs. Thus, medical relief agencies agreed to include this kind of activity in order to be able to carry out their intended nutrition programs.

The withdrawal of these organizations, as noted above, was mainly due to the specific prerequisites of medical humanitarian assistance. Direct contact with patients, for instance, is indispensable if one carries out therapeutic feeding programs. In agricultural rehabilitation programs, in contrast, the international staff communicates with technical staff, farmers, directors of cooperative farms, and so forth. An agency active in this field is thus able to make more compromises concerning access to individual beneficiaries than an organization of medical doctors who intend to treat patients. In addition, the experience of European NGOs shows that agencies working in the agricultural sector succeed more easily in improving their relationships with North Korean authorities and local staff. Agencies such as GAA report that their interlocutors are indeed very interested in modern cultivation methods and technologies. In contrast, medical relief agencies report that they have not succeeded in establishing a relationship of trust with their interlocutors and national staff. Authorities do not seem to be very interested in the agencies' knowledge of malnutrition treatment or medical care in general.

Furthermore, local staff members of GAA and other agriculture-oriented NGOs have seldom been changed by the FDRC. Cap Anamur, which focuses on the rehabilitation of health and children's institutions, has also experienced a steady improvement in its relationship with North Korean authorities. Medical organizations, however, complain that their local staff members have been replaced at relatively short intervals.

In short, the fact that agricultural rehabilitation has largely replaced medical assistance is due to two factors: the characteristics of medical agencies and their work on the one hand, and the North Korean government's obvious priorities on the other.[34]

For agricultural recovery programs, the main goal is mid-term increases in food production. Double-cropping programs seem to be a particular priority for the FDRC. It appeared to international aid workers that a top-level decision was made in 1997–98 that advocated the planting of crops that allow two harvests a year. Double-cropping programs require some external input (barley seeds, fertilizer) and thus became a door opener for international aid agencies. Within their space of maneuverability, NGOs and UN agencies try to gradually convince their North Korean counterparts to adopt some strategies of sustainable cultivation methods (diversification of crops, reduction of pesticides, etc.). In a sense, double-cropping has been a two-sided issue. On the one hand, it has allowed aid agencies to get their feet in the door. On the other hand, aid agencies advocate a shift in agricultural policy toward more sustainable cultivation methods; double-cropping means further intensifying the use of soils.

Using the terms of Noland, Robinson, and Wang, the DPRK government theoretically has four options in dealing with the food crisis: a production-oriented strategy, an aid-oriented strategy, a trade-oriented strategy, and a reform-oriented strategy.[35] In light of European NGO experience gained over the past six years, it appears evident that the government sees an increase in food production as the most appropriate way out of the crisis.[36]

Insights into the Current Situation

Visiting the DPRK or being stationed in the country is not tantamount to having deep insight into North Korean society. On field trips, national staff and/or FDRC officials always escort humanitarian workers. In general, no direct or unfiltered communication with ordinary people is possible, and sites for field visits cannot be selected randomly. Permanent international staff are lodged in Pyongyang's diplomatic quarter, called by aid workers "the diplomatic zoo." During field trips or while based in sub-offices outside Pyongyang, aid workers are subject to particularly tight restrictions on liberty of movement. Therefore, aid agencies—resident or nonresident—are not able to draw a complete picture of North Korea's internal situation. Yet to a limited extent, their experiences and observations throw light on some aspects of the reality in North Korea.

Even regarding the very reason for their presence in the country—the humanitarian crisis—aid agencies have no definitive information. While NGO delegations were invited to visit potential project sites before the establishment of a program, comprehensive assessment studies outside the UN-led crop assessments could not be conducted. As a result, European NGOs issued contradictory statements on whether there is a famine in North Korea. In 1997, GAA's annual report stated that the entire country was hit by a famine. Yet according to an MSF medical doctor who returned from a mission in 1998, the situation in North Korea does not allow one to speak of a famine.[37]

In general, aid agencies in North Korea are in no position to completely assess the population's humanitarian needs. The extent of the crisis and mortality rates are better estimated by outside observers who have access to a wider range of information sources.[38] But it is noteworthy that European NGOs saw few acutely malnourished people, or dead bodies, in the streets. Medical relief organizations did report in their preimplementation assessment missions that they saw some severely malnourished children in institutions. As noted above, only a few acutely malnourished children have been seen in institutions visited over the course of the projects.

As for the state of the country's agriculture, NGOs have a better, yet still incomplete, picture. Wide deforestation and an increasing number of small pieces of privately cultivated land covering more or less arable land are evident. The lack of agricultural inputs, energy, and spare parts have forced agriculture to make a leap back in time to preindustrialization. In cooperative farms visited by European NGOs, plows pulled by oxen have replaced tractors.

Labor seems to be abundant. Aid workers frequently question whether the deployment of laborers corresponds to the size of the task. Sometimes numerous people are seen cleaning a street or a building very thoroughly with minimal tools, such that one gets the impression of people just being occupied.

Moreover, the system that used to provide a link between food-producing and food-consuming populations evidently has collapsed. In 1995 and 1996, the urban population assisted farmers in seeding and harvest seasons. People either walked or were transported in buses from the cities to the agricultural regions; it was an event that had a bit of the character of a parish fair, both visible and audible to outsiders. In recent years, however, the columns of urban people assisting the rural population have vanished from the streets. Instead, columns of farmers and their family members can be seen on their way into the cities carrying agricultural products. Markets reportedly have been set up, tolerated, and controlled by the authorities. International NGO staff members are not permitted to visit these markets and thus cannot estimate their importance, number, or the prices of products. But given the aforementioned observations, one can assume that markets have replaced the former system of interaction between food producers and the rest of the population.

The political situation is very hard to assess, given the living and working conditions of aid agency staff in North Korea. Yet it is clear that no aid agencies have witnessed any uproar or turmoil, as reported by some authors.[39] The main interlocutors for international staff are representatives of North Korean authorities who hardly make any political, let alone critical, statements.

In general, a state's inability to feed its population poses a risk to the political leadership's legitimacy. According to a classical definition, "legitimacy involves the capacity of a political system to engender and maintain the belief that existing political institutions are the most appropriate or proper ones for the society."[40] With regard to the North Korean state propagating autarky and self-reliance, depending on foreign food aid is a particularly delicate issue. Although on a working level, North Korean staff express their gratitude to international aid agencies, the official propaganda illustrates that the reception of aid is seen as ideologically problematic.[41] The experience of aid agencies in the DPRK reveals that the authorities make an effort to keep knowledge about the aid to a minimum.

As noted above, working and living conditions hinder the ability of aid agencies to be in contact with ordinary North Koreans. In addition, the origin of aid items is generally not evident to the individual beneficiary. At first, labels identifying the South Korean origin of noodle packages were scratched off, ships carrying the Republic of Korea (ROK) flag were not permitted to enter North Korean harbors,[42] and bags filled with donated food appeared to be turned inside out to hide the UN or U.S. logo. In recent years, however, identification labels have been more accepted, although explanations in Korean are rare.

European NGOs supporting cooperative farms or health institutions predominantly assume that individual beneficiaries are not aware of the origin of the aid. Institution staff, farmers, and other direct interlocutors, however, know that the support is provided by an organization from a foreign country.

In general, NGOs working along the Chinese border, where they have direct contact with North Korean refugees, have better access to information on public opinion in the DPRK. According to some studies, criticisms of the political leadership, as well as knowledge about the existence of international aid, are spreading.[43]

NORTH KOREA'S APPROACH TO HANDLING EUROPEAN NGOS

The Flood Damage Rehabilitation Committee

With the exception of HI, which is collaborating with the Korean Association for Supporting the Disabled, all European NGOs are dealing with the North Korean FDRC. The FDRC was created in 1995 under the North Korean Ministry of Foreign Affairs. The fact that the Ministry of Foreign Affairs is in charge of dealing with humanitarian NGOs distinguishes North Korea from many other countries that receive international aid. In most cases, NGOs are used to dealing with line ministries, such as public health or agriculture. In North Korea, however, durable, longer-term relationships with institutions other than the FDRC—such as line ministries or academic associations—are very difficult to establish.

According to the country's administrative structure, the FDRC is present on the community, provincial, and national level. Thus, the FDRC is also the interlocutor for daily work issues. FDRC staff are mostly officials from the Ministry of Foreign Affairs or from provincial or district authorities. Therefore, FDRC staff lack the technical knowledge often required to deal with NGO concerns adequately. MSF, for instance, was frequently frustrated in discussions of medical issues with the FDRC.

European NGOs get in touch with North Korean line ministries only on an ad hoc basis, mainly on field trips where, in addition to the FDRC, other institutions and authorities are represented. International staff have had the experience that representatives from the Ministry of Food, Agriculture, or Public Health show strong interest in technical issues in direct conversations with humanitarian workers. According to the reports of some NGOs, technical, nondiplomatic staff do not show this interest in the presence of FDRC representatives.

Communication between the FDRC and other institutions and authorities seems to be rather limited, at least as far as NGO requests are concerned. Aid agencies report that their requests are rarely handed over horizontally from one authority to another. The central agent for NGO concerns remains the FDRC.

All in all, the FDRC is perceived by European NGOs as an obstacle rather than a counterpart. Accordingly, the EC, in preparation for a top-level visit to Pyongyang in May 2001, formulated a briefing note for the commissioner in charge of external relations: "NGOs should gain access to technical line ministries and institutions and the FDRC should really work as a facilitator, not as a stumbling block."[44]

Negotiation Processes

Each aid agency's engagement in the DPRK is based on a letter of under-standing negotiated with the FDRC. According to European NGOs, negotiating with the FDRC is a unique experience. NGOs are faced with what an NGO repre-sentative calls an "obsessive level of detail." Lengthy discussions surround details that in all other countries are not part of written agreements. In a 17-page contract between MDM and the FDRC, for instance, even the price for the petrol used by MDM vehicles is fixed.

Much has been written about the great importance Asian cultures attach to saving face. Within the context of negotiations, saving face means avoiding the "humiliation of having to admit weaknesses or failures in one's position."[45] In North Korea, this approach is particularly important—and difficult for west-erners to understand. Aid agencies report that even facts and numbers—the output of an energy plant or a water pump—have been a matter of negotiation. North Korean staff have given figures that have evidently collided with the less rosy reality. Thus, fact-finding missions have ended up bargaining with institu-tion staff. This has been a new experience even for aid workers with extensive experience in other Asian countries.

Of particular importance is the decision-making structure of the North Korean side. Three levels of interaction between aid agencies and North Korean coun-terparts can be distinguished. The first level can be described as the *working level,* where international aid workers have limited contact with farmers or insti-tution staff in order to address technical issues. This level has no relevant decision-making power.

The communication with FDRC representatives in the context of project design, as well as working and monitoring conditions, is the second level, the *negotiation level.* This level is the main area of communication and negotiation between aid agencies and the North Korean side. Significantly—and surprisingly to NGO representatives—this level has only very limited decision-making power over the issues on the agenda. It appears that North Korean negotiators' main task consists primarily of transferring information to the next decision-making level. This seems to be established practice, particularly when it comes to issues of major importance, such as the location of programs, the designation of insti-tutions and target groups, or the number of expatriate staff. Consequently, NGOs have had the frustrating experience where the seeming nodding in agreement of FDRC representatives at the negotiation table turns out to be meaningless at the following meeting.

Negotiated positions and NGO requests are transferred to the third level, the *decision-making level.* This level formulates positions and negotiation targets and decides whether an NGO request is refused or accepted. Significantly, this level cannot be assigned to a specific level within the FDRC or any other insti-tution. The decision-making level is always the one higher than the negotiation level. If negotiations proceed on the district level, decisions will be taken on the provincial level. If the provincial FDRC is the negotiator, the decision-making level will be the FDRC in Pyongyang. As one aid worker said, "Should you ever be permitted to negotiate with the minister, you can be sure that decisions will be taken by Kim Jong Il himself."

Negotiators and decisionmakers are separate individuals or groups of people. Consequently, establishing a relationship of trust with negotiators and interlocutors generally has no short-term impact on such relevant issues as an agency's maneuverability or access to information. Reported improvements largely concern issues that are within the negotiation level's limited competence. This progress includes permission for an aid worker to take a walk in the hotel area without escort or permission for a medical doctor to carry out an operation by him- or herself. The decision-making structure within the North Korean administration hinders any fundamental short-term change for the better in terms of working conditions for humanitarian agencies.

A better understanding of humanitarian work and the building of mutual trust might turn out in the long term to be an effective means for improving working conditions for aid workers in North Korea. Encouraging progress in this respect has been made by numerous aid agencies in the past. No consistency, however, in dealing with European NGOs can be detected. Instead, NGOs claim that progress largely depends on the people involved and personal relationships. Given North Korea's history, its cultural settings, and its administration's decision-making structure, more patience is needed here, arguably, than in any other part of the world. Many European aid workers are prepared to invest this patience, counting on a gradual improvement of the North Korean population's humanitarian situation. The patience of those who see their task as the immediate saving of human lives, however, has been exhausted.

NGO ADVOCACY AND NORTH KOREAN POLICY EVOLUTION

In contrast to U.S., South Korean, and Japanese aid agencies, European NGOs have taken differing stands on policies toward North Korea. Questions concerning the effects of aid to the DPRK and the role of aid agencies have split the European NGO community into two groups: a small group of large NGOs and a large group of smaller NGOs.

The "Hard Landing" Strategy

The first position—publicly advocated by MSF and ACF, and in large part also shared by MDM and Oxfam—questions whether assistance to North Korea even makes sense. In the view of these organizations, international aid does not reach those in greatest need. Moreover, the aid is a kind of perversion, in effect stabilizing the totalitarian regime and "feeding the dictator."[46] This group of aid agencies therefore argues that NGOs find themselves in an awkward position: The North Korean government uses humanitarian aid to stabilize its power, which, by extension, is also seen as a goal pursued by western donors with their so-called "soft-landing" strategy.

The criticism from this NGO group focuses on the DPRK government's practice of food distribution and aid agencies' head-in-the-sand "ostrich politics" in North Korea.[47] The PDS is seen as the main instrument of control. François Jean from MSF-France has argued that the PDS must be seen in the context of the classification system of North Korean society, in which an individual's status is determined by his or her political loyalty and that of his or her ancestors.[48] Since all food aid is channeled through the PDS, "it has become part of the system of oppression."[49]

The allegation that international aid is not distributed in accordance with humanitarian principles is not directed only at the DPRK government. According to ACF and MSF, the weak stand on international principles taken by some NGOs—in particular, UN agencies—has led to "humanitarian dumping"[50] in North Korea. In this view, "to make gifts without any effective control over them" is seen as "most certainly detrimental to humanitarian aid as a whole."[51]

In sum, a number of the biggest European NGOs have concluded that a common and firmer stand by aid agencies in North Korea is required in order to push through respect for humanitarian principles. However, "humanitarian aid is not possible everywhere," as noted by the president of MSF-France, who referred to the role the ICRC played during the holocaust.[52]

In accordance with this critical analysis of humanitarian action in the DPRK, these NGOs are extremely skeptical about North Korea's integration into the international community. In particular, they believe that integration, reconciliation, and peace are political goals that should be achieved by political actors. Conversely, from the perspective mainly of medical relief organizations, the humanitarian mandate obliges aid agencies to carry out the apolitical work of bringing relief to the suffering without advancing political interests.[53]

In a broader perspective, all European NGOs acknowledge that political and diplomatic engagement is the only means to achieve change in North Korea. Establishing diplomatic ties, however, is seen by MSF as "bestowing legitimacy on Kim Jong Il and his clique."[54] Massive human rights violations are brought forward as the main argument against the establishment of diplomatic relations. Both before and after its withdrawal, MSF reported on the human rights situation in the DPRK. Its information source was interviews with North Korean refugees in the Chinese border area.[55]

The argument that the human rights situation in North Korea does not allow the establishment of full diplomatic relations is also put forward by the governments of France and the Republic of Ireland. To date, all other EU member states have decided to establish diplomatic ties with the DPRK.

Change Through Rapprochement

"Change through rapprochement" (*"Wandel durch Annäherung"*) was the guiding principle of West German Chancellor Willy Brandt's *Ostpolitik*. It accurately describes the policy advocated by those European NGOs still providing aid to North Korea.

As opposed to the first group of aid agencies, the remaining European NGOs working in the country are more reluctant to issue public statements or articles on the political environment of aid distribution in North Korea. Although their views on the alleged abuses of food aid vary, these agencies do not question the sense of distributing the aid. Some share the criticism of the government's distribution practices; others regard the PDS as an efficient and reliable distribution mechanism. Some agree that UN agencies are "too diplomatic" in their negotiations with the DPRK government and thus undermine the NGOs' positions. Others praise UN coordination efforts and UN agencies' steady—though not publicly visible—insistence on international working standards. The main point is that this group of agencies claims that assistance to North Korea is not only a matter of humanitarian impact but also of longer-term socio-political effects.

The aid projects' impact (as noted above, now mainly rehabilitation programs) is generally perceived as very positive. A further reason for staying in North Korea is the perception that NGOs are a "bridge" between North Korea and the outside world. Improvements in the relationship with North Korean staff are perceived as signs of a better understanding of the work of NGOs.

From 1995 to 2000, European NGOs provided important contact between North Korea and western donor governments. In a sense, NGOs did pave the way for the establishment of diplomatic relations between the DPRK and 13 EU member states. All European NGOs currently providing assistance to North Korea have welcomed this development. Addressing structural problems in North Korea through rehabilitation and development aid is also advocated by these NGOs. From this perspective, the further integration of the DPRK with international fora and organizations is seen as significant progress.

The argument that, through their continued efforts, European NGOs contribute to a better relationship between North Korea and the international community is also shared by the most important donor to this group, the EC. Thus, humanitarian need is seen as one important reason to help North Korea; the other, as one EC official put it, is the opportunity to "open their minds." In other words, the aim is to gradually create a situation in which the labeling of aid workers as "imperialists and crafty plunderers"[56] finds no support in North Korea. Under this logic, NGOs—through their mere presence, their work, and the principles of their actions—provide a counter-example to the world picture still propagated in North Korea. In that sense, the concrete goals of assistance, whether relief, rehabilitation, or structural reform, are secondary.

NOTES

1. Alain Destexhe, *L'humanitaire impossible ou deux siècles d'ambiguïté* [*The Impossible Humanitarian or Two Centuries of Ambiguity*] (Paris: Armand Colin, 1993), p. 69. (All translations from the French are the author's.)

2. Rony Brauman, *L'action humanitaire* [*The Humanitarian Action*] (Paris: Flammarion, 1995), p. 60. For an overview of the founding history of French medical NGOs, see Johanna Siméant, "Entrer, rester en humanitaire: des fondateurs de MSF aux membres actuels des ONG médicales françaises" ["To Enter into and to Remain in Humanitarianism: From the Founders of MSF to the Present French Medical NGOs"], *Revue française de science politique* [*The French Review of Political Science*] 51, no. 1-2 (February-April 2001): 47–72.

3. Francis Sejersted (lecture given in Oslo, Norway, 10 December 1999). Mr. Sejersted was chairman of the Norwegian Nobel Committee.

4. FAO/WFP, *Special Report: Crop and Food Supply Assessment Mission to the Democratic People's Republic of Korea,* 29 June 1999.

5. FAO/WFP, *Special Report: Crop and Food Supply Assessment Mission to the Democratic People's Republic of Korea,* 8 November 1999, p. 9.

6. Jon Bennett, *North Korea: The Politics of Food Aid,* RRN Network Paper, no. 28 (London: Overseas Development Institute, 1999), p. 19.

7. *Libération* (Paris), 11 July 1998.

8. *Libération* (Paris), 11 July 1998.

9. For details, see *Messages: Journal interne des Médecins Sans Frontières,* no. 101, November 1998, p. 2.

10. See IFRC, *World Disaster Report 2000* (Oxford: Oxford University Press, 2000), p. 84.

11. EU, UNICEF, and WFP, *Nutrition Survey of the Democratic People's Republic of Korea,* report on a study undertaken in collaboration with the DPRK government, November 1998. The study concluded that 62 percent of children ages six months to seven years are chronically malnourished, 16 percent severely.

12. Anne Scheppen, "Viele kommen, einer geht" ["Many are coming, one is leaving"], Frankfurter Allgemeine Zeitung, 27 September 2002.

13. See note 12.

14. United Nations Economic and Social Council, *Economic, Social, and Cultural Rights: The Right to Food,* document no. E/CN.4/2001/53, 7 February 2001, p. 11.

15. Doug Struck, "U.N. Says Aid Averted a North Korean Famine," *Washington Post,* 24 August 2001.

16. Catherine Bertini, *Agence France-Presse* (Geneva), 7 June 2001.

17. Christophe Reltien, "Humanitarian Action in North Korea: Ostrich Politics," in *The Geopolitics of Hunger: Hunger and Power,* ed. Action Against Hunger (Boulder, Colo.: Lynne Rienner, 2001), p. 163.

18. A bilateral agreement between the DPRK and the German government, for instance, negotiated prior to the establishment of diplomatic relations in March 2001, contained some improvements in German NGOs' working conditions. According to these aid agencies, however, this agreement had no concrete impact on their work in North Korea.

19. European Commission, *Linking Relief, Rehabilitation, and Development,* communication from the EC, 30 April 1996.

20. Mary B. Anderson, *Do No Harm: How Aid Can Support Peace—or War.* (Boulder, Colo.: Lynne Rienner, 1999), p. 146.

21. For a discussion of development aid in the DPRK, see also Erich Weingartner, *NGO Contributions to DPRK Development: Issues for Canada and the International Community.* North Pacific Policy Papers, no. 7. (Vancouver, BC: Program on Canada-Asia Policy Studies/Institute of Asian Research, 2001).

22. See Michael Schloms, "Humanitarianism and Peace. On the (Im-)possible Inclusion of Humanitarian Assistance into Peacebuilding Efforts," *Journal of Humanitarian Assistance* (www.jha.ac/articles/a072.htm, posted 9 October 2001).

23. Bennett, North Korea, p. 4, note 6.

24. In November 2001, only 3.6 percent of FAO/UNDP appeals were covered, versus 69.6 percent of WFP programs. See UN OCHA, *DPRKorea Situation Bulletin,* no. 9/01 (October 2001).

25. See Marcus Noland, *Avoiding the Apocalypse: The Future of the Two Koreas* (Washington, DC: Institute for International Economics, 2000).

26. For details on North Korea's trade with the Soviet Union, see Nicholas Eberstadt, Marc Rubin, and Albina Tretyakova, "The Collapse of Soviet and Russian Trade with the DPRK, 1989–1993: Impact and Implications," *Korean Journal of National Reunification* 4 (1995): 88–193. For the DPRK's trade with mainland China, see Banning Garrett and Bonnie Glaser, "Looking Across the Yalu: Chinese Assessments of North Korea," *Asian Survey* 35, no. 6 (1995), 528–546.

27. See, *inter alia,* Heather Smith and Yiping Huang, "Achieving Food Security in North Korea," in *Promoting International Scientific, Technological and Economic Cooperation in the Korean Peninsula: Enhancing Stability and International Dialogue,* eds. Paolo Cotta-Ramusino and Maurizio Martellini (Como, Italy: Landau Network – Centro Volta, 2000), pp. 201–218.

28. Marcus Noland, Sherman Robinson, and Tao Wang, *Famine in North Korea: Causes and Cures,* Working Paper 99-2 (Washington, DC: Institute for International Economics, 1999), p. 22. See also Kwon Tae-jin and Kim Woon-keun, "Assessment of Food Supply in North Korea," *Journal of Rural Development* 22 (1999): 47–66. Page 62: "[T]he required inputs cannot be available on a sustainable basis without the development of a national capacity to import." Smith and Huang (2000) come to a very similar conclusion: "North Korea's famine represents a classic case of food insecurity arising from a strategy of self-reliance. To achieve food security over the longer term, North Korea must start to adjust its economic structure in light of its own comparative advantages and increase its interactions with the international markets" (p. 211, note 27).

29. An EU-funded project would be unique in the program landscape. In May 2001, North Korean officials told a high-level EU delegation in Pyongyang that North Korea is interested in training courses in market economies, the energy sector, and modern agriculture. Meanwhile, the EU agreed to establish an educational program funded with 5 million euros.

30. See note 4.

31. Noland (2000), note 25, p. 282.

32. See, for instance, the comments of Lim Dong-won, South Korean presidential adviser on national security and foreign policy: "North Korea appears to be moving toward a market economy, following in the steps of China." Quoted in *Agence France-Presse,* "North Korea carrying out free-market economic reform: South Korea," 25 July 2002.

33. See Bennett, *North Korea,* p. 19, note 6, and Kevin M. Cahill, "Clinical Aspects of Famine," in *A Framework for Survival: Health, Human Rights, and Humanitarian Assistance in Conflicts and Disasters,* ed. Kevin M. Cahill (New York, London: Routledge and the Center for International Health and Cooperation, 1999), pp. 26–30.

34. The DPRK finance minister announced in 1999 that agriculture and electric power are the government's priorities. See Economist Intelligence Unit (EIU), *EIU Country Report. South Korea/North Korea* (London: EIU, Second Quarter 1999), p. 41.

35. See note 28.

36. See Michael Schloms, "Zwischen Gesichtsverlust und Machterhalt—Der nordkoreanische Staat und sein Umgang mit der Hungerkrise" ["Between the Loss of Face and Power Maintenance—The North Korean State and its Handling of the Food Crisis"], in

Korea 2001: Politik, Wirtschaft, Gesellschaft [Korea 2001: Politics, Economy, Society] ed. Patrick Köllner (Hamburg: Institute for Asian Studies, 2001), pp. 192–213.

37. See the MSF report "Corée: Les hôpitaux sont de grandes boîtes vides" ["Korea: The Hospitals are Large, Empty Boxes"], in *Messages. Journal Interne des Médecins Sans Frontières* 97 (March 1998): 6.

38. A recent study estimates the number of famine-related deaths from 1995 to 2000 to be between 600,000 and 1 million. See Daniel Goodkind and Loraine West "The North Korean Famine and Its Demographic Impact," *Population and Development Review* 27, no. 2 (2001). For a study on mortality in northern regions of the DPRK, see W. Courtland Robinson, Myung Ken Lee, Kenneth Hill, and Gilbert M. Burnham, "Mortality in North Korean Migrant Households: A Retrospective Study," *The Lancet* 354 (1999): 291–295.

39. Don Oberdorfer, *The Two Koreas* (Reading, Mass.: Addison-Wesley, 1997), p. 375: "In the early fall [of 1995], the Korean People's Army Sixth Corps, in the northeastern part of the country, was disbanded, its leadership purged, and its units submerged into others, under circumstances suggesting disarray in the ranks."

40. Martin Lipset, "Some Social Requisites of Democracy: Economic Development and Political Legitimacy," *American Political Science Review* 53 (1959): 68.

41. In an article on aid provided by western donors, the Rodong Sinmun concludes "wishing or asking for 'aid' and 'cooperation' from the imperialists leads to national subordination and ruin." 22 July 2001.

42. See Noland, Robinson, and Wang, *Famine in North Korea,* p. 10, note 28.

43. See Philo Kim, "The Sociopolitical Impact of the Food Crisis in North Korea," *Korea and World Affairs* 23, no. 2 (1999): 207–224. Kim reports that in a study undertaken in spring 1998, only 20 percent of 850 interviewed refugees blamed the food crisis on climatic factors. Forty-five percent said the crisis was due to the government, Kim Jong Il, the bureaucracy, or the lack of political and economic reform (p. 220). See Good Friends, *Report on Daily Life and Human Rights of North Korean Displaced Persons in China* (Seoul: Good Friends/Center for Peace, Human Rights, and Refugees, 1999).

44. Quoted in Giorgio Maragliano, paper presented at the Third International NGO Conference on Humanitarian Assistance to North Korea, Seoul, Republic of Korea, Annex 2, 17–20 June 2001.

45. Scott Snyder, *Negotiating on the Edge. North Korean Negotiating Behavior* (Washington, DC: United States Institute of Peace, 1999), p. 89.

46. Fiona Terry, "Feeding the Dictator," *The Guardian* (London), 6 August 2001.

47. Reltien, "Humanitarian Action in North Korea," p. 166, note 17.

48. François Jean, "Corée du Nord: Un régime de famine" ["North Korea: A Regime of Famine"], *Esprit* 2 (1999) : 23.

49. Terry, "Feeding the Dictator," note 46.

50. ACF, "Action Contre la Faim décide de se retirer de Corée du Nord" ["Action Against Hunger Decides to Pull Out of North Korea"], *Journal d'ACF,* no. 7, March 2000): 13. See also Sylvie Brunel, "Corée du Nord: une famine virtuelle?" ["North Korea: A Virtual Famine?"] in *Géopolitique de la faim. Quand la faim est une arme. [Geopolitics of Hunger: When Hunger Is a Weapon],* ed. Action Contre la Faim (Paris: Presses Universitaires de France, 1998), pp. 132–138.

51. Reltien, "Humanitarian Action in North Korea," p. 166, note 17.

52. Jean-Hervé Bradol (president of MSF-France) and Christiane Bertiaume (spokesperson of WFP), interview broadcast by the French radio station RMC Info, 24 August 2001.

53. See James Orbinski (president of MSF International): "In the vast majority of situations where humanitarian need arises out of political turmoil, there is, obviously, an inherently political context you have to operate in. This does not, however, mean you have to succumb to the desire of the various political forces to influence your choice and your delivery of humanitarian action." *World Disaster Report,* p. 84, note 10.

54. Terry, "Feeding the Dictator," note 46.
55. For example, see *MSF Newsletter* 41 (3 September 2001).
56. Rodong Sinmun, 22 July 2001.

Chapter Four
The Role of South Korea's NGOs: The Political Context

Chung Oknim

INTRODUCTION

The volatile security situation on the Korean Peninsula has led the governments of the two Koreas to tightly control dialogue and exchanges between Pyongyang and Seoul during the past half century. In the South, unauthorized contacts with North Korea were punishable under the National Security Law. In the North, political control over Democratic People's Republic of Korea (DPRK) citizens was paramount as part of the overarching control of the socialist state and, more recently, the effort to ensure regime survival. And yet, the Korean Peninsula, divided by ideological, political, and physical boundaries, remains ethnically homogeneous despite the long division and continues to share deep emotional ties. South Korea's assistance to North Korea has been shaped by this political and social complexity, and thus cannot be described as merely a humanitarian gesture. The bitter history of the Korean War and the Cold War structure continue to define relations between North and South Korea even today. The hostility that has dominated their relations also reflects the conservative nature of those who have held power or shaped opinions in both societies. As a result, South Korea's laws and institutions, as well as its broader international perceptions, have blocked more frequent exchanges and contacts between North and South Korea.

When widespread flooding struck North Korea in August 1995, the country's permanent representative to its United Nations mission in New York pleaded for help from the UN Department of Humanitarian Affairs (UNDHA) and the rest of the world. The plea was noted with sympathetic interest in South Korea, particularly among religious groups. Up to that time, the South Korean government's policy on North Korea had been constrained by two variables—the regional security environment and domestic politics. Thus, the South Korean government found it difficult to authorize assistance to North Korea out of concern for the possible impact on domestic politics. Private organizations found that they could work only within a very limited scope. The issues of whether and how to provide assistance to the North were also closely linked with the North Korea policies of both President Kim Young Sam and his successor Kim Dae Jung, uniquely shaping the humanitarian response of South Korean nongovernmental organizations (NGOs) that wished to undertake projects in the North. Because of these impediments, it took a relatively long time to institutionalize the process of providing assistance to North Korea. When action was taken, however, it motivated South Koreans to take a greater interest in their brethren (a.k.a., main enemy) in the North. Gradually, however, consultations and information exchanges among private organizations and coordination with South Korea's Ministry of Unification began to take place. Over time, these efforts led to an expansion of activities, starting with general relief operations and evolving into capacity-building projects.

The South Korean NGOs have differences in their origins and evolution compared with NGOs in the United States or Europe. They tend to have a more optimistic prism through which they observe internal dynamism and possibilities for change in North Korea. They put more emphasis on confidence-building through frequent contacts than on hewing closely to humanitarian principles. For South Korean NGOs, nationalism, unification, and reconciliation are the main motivations for relief activities that extend beyond simple humanitarianism. In sharp contrast with U.S. and European NGOs, which have experienced frustration and donor fatigue and have reduced their activities in the North, South Korean NGOs have broadened the scope of their activities and number of contacts since 2000, albeit on a relatively small scale.

INTER-KOREAN RELATIONS AND THE "ANT CORPS" CAMPAIGN [1]

With the advent of the post–Cold War era, relations among South Korea, the United States, and North Korea developed into an awkward triangle. Seoul was openly uneasy about dialogue between Washington and Pyongyang. This uneasiness included South Korean feelings about the Geneva Agreement (Agreed Framework) concluded by the United States and North Korea in October 1994 to resolve the North Korean nuclear issue. South Korea felt isolated from the U.S.-DPRK talks—the Republic of Korea (ROK) government had planned to hold its own talks with the DPRK and resented having been excluded. (In an attempt to block the U.S.-North Korea talks, South Korean intelligence reported dubious allegations by North Korean defector Kang Myung-do [who claimed to be a son-in-law of North Korea's then-Prime Minister Kang Sung-san] that North Korea had already developed five nuclear weapons.[2]) In fact, South Korean President Kim Young Sam was eager to have talks with his counterpart in Pyongyang. When former U.S. President Jimmy Carter visited North Korea in June 1994 and conveyed to Seoul then-North Korean leader Kim Il Sung's proposal for an inter-Korean summit, he accepted without hesitation. Indeed, over the years, successive

South Korean governments have been acutely aware of the potential impact of inter-Korean talks on domestic politics and security on the peninsula. Therefore, the South has never hesitated to seize an opportunity to engage in such talks.

President Kim Young Sam had delivered a speech in Berlin less than six months before the flooding in North Korea declaring his willingness to provide grain to the North on generous terms. The South's Ministry of Unification made follow-up calls for dialogue on the proposed food donation and expressed its willingness to provide grain with no strings attached.[3]

These activities culminated in June 1995 in inter-Korean governmental talks held for the first time in Beijing, during which the Seoul government agreed to provide 150,000 tons of rice to North Korea. The South's Lee Suk-chae, vice minister of finance and economy, and the North's Chun Kum-chul, chairman of that country's Asia Pacific Peace Committee (APPC), led the negotiations.[4]

A donation of $232 million (185.4 billion won) was made through the South Korean government's North-South Cooperation Fund to cover the costs of the shipment of rice in unmarked bags by boat from South Korea to the North. In July of 1995, the second round of inter-Korean governmental talks was held in Beijing to discuss the direct provision of the promised aid.

When the devastation caused by the 1995 floods was reported in the international media, six leading religious groups in South Korea established the Pan-Religious Order Promotion Committee to Help Our North Korean Brethren. At that time, the Kim Young Sam administration took a passive attitude toward the campaign, making it virtually impossible to use government funds for relief efforts. The passivity can be partly explained by hard-line criticisms of the 1994 U.S.-DPRK Agreed Framework and by Kim Young Sam's lingering resentment over not having been included in the talks. Moreover, the sudden death of the North Korean leader, Kim Il Sung, meant that the planned summit meeting (arranged by former U.S. President Jimmy Carter) never took place.

In addition, other domestic political issues linked to inter-Korean relations—including elections and public opinion, as well as the roles and interests of surrounding powers—also had a dampening effect on intergovernmental talks between the two Koreas. The pressure these issues created restrained the activities of private relief organizations that wanted to respond to the floods. Direct assistance from the South to the North was also delayed by several inter-Korean incidents, including the hoisting of the North Korean flag on a South Korean ship transporting food for the North, the detention of the crew of the South Korean ship *Samson Venus* on the grounds that crew members took pictures of the North Korean port of Chungjin, and the repatriation issue of the crew of the kidnapped South Korean ship *Woosung*. Consequently, the South Korean government decided that any future humanitarian aid to the North should be undertaken only through the Korean Red Cross. It called for a reduction in donations—a move met with strong resistance from South Korea's NGOs.[5]

In reality, the "single-channel" policy for humanitarian assistance was put forward by the South Korean authorities to prevent both frequent contact with

North Korea and the development of competition in providing aid to the North. A clear departure from the voluntary spirit of civic movements, the government's strictures created antagonism and conflict between the government and the NGO sector.[6]

Meanwhile, South Korean religious groups organized a Peace Conference in January 1996 to plead for assistance for the North Korean flood victims. In March of the same year, civilian organizations launched a public campaign to help North Koreans. In June 1996, seven organizations held a mass to call for a multiple-channel aid policy that would include NGO contributions, instead of the single Red Cross channel monopolized by the governments. The group also asked for government permission to send rice to the famine-stricken North. As a result, the Korean Sharing Movement (KSM), led by social groups of the religious orders, was launched for the purpose of assisting North Koreans and pursuing national reconciliation.[7]

KSM's main goal was to help North Koreans; the group also, however, promoted exchange projects by supporting overseas ethnic Koreans in the Korean autonomous region in Yanbian, China, and the Korean community in Vladivostok, Russia.[8] The KSM collected donations through public campaigns, attracting public attention to the issue of assisting South Korea's Northern counterparts. KSM provided 50,000 bags of flour to North Korea, a project in which 33 people representing six religious orders and civilian organizations played a major role.[9]

The Korean Red Cross arranged the delivery of the relief materials, and the International Federation of Red Cross and Red Crescent Societies (IFRC) delivered them by ship to the North Korean port of Nampo via the South Korean port of Inchon. From July 1995 to May 1997, the South Korean Red Cross collected $4.96 million in civilian relief goods, which were delivered to North Korea by the IFRC (an agreement between the North and South Korean Red Cross organizations on direct delivery had been reached earlier in the month[10]).

Beginning in 1996, additional private organizations formed to assist North Korea began to pop up, and soon relief aid to the North was in full swing, having been positioned as a civic campaign in South Korea. In addition to KSM, Medical Aid for Children of the D.P.R.Korea (1997), the Eugene Bell Centennial Foundation (EBCF, 1996), and the Korea Welfare Foundation (KWF, 1991) launched official assistance projects for North Korea in the health care and medical sectors.

However, North Korea's submarine incursion into South Korean waters in September 1996 strained not only inter-Korean relations but also the ability of various NGO relief projects to go forward with North Korean aid projects. Political circles and the general public in South Korea were in an uproar—to such an extent that no view other than a Korean version of McCarthyism had any chance of being heard. Even Kim Dae Jung—then leader of the major opposition party, National Congress for New Politics—participated in a rally to condemn North Korea. The Kim Young Sam government made it clear that it would suspend any aid to the North that had not passed through government-level nego-tiations until there was a visible change in North Korea's attitude. However, as a way of showing flexibility, the South Korean government did not stop aiding the North through international organizations such as the United Nations (UN) World Food Program (WFP) and the UN Children's Fund (UNICEF). In December 1996, the Humanitarian Affairs Bureau was established within the Ministry of Unification. The bureau took full responsibility for humanitarian aid to North Korea. When North Korea officially apologized for its submarine infiltration into Kangneung, South Korea, the ROK government resumed relief aid to the North through the South Korean National Red Cross.[11]

KSM stressed the importance of efforts to seek peace under these strained condi-tions and arranged a massive campaign that included declarations on the state of the nation, discussions, and debates about aiding North Koreans in order to bring change to the policy environment as well as public opinion. In 1997, international organizations and Koreans living in Yanbian and Manchuria revealed that North Korea's food distribution system, also known as the Public Distribution System (PDS), had collapsed. To raise public awareness about the calamity, KSM invited staff members from EBCF and the World Council of Churches (WCC) to hold an international congress on the food crisis in North Korea in March 1997. This was part of KSM's effort to favorably influence public opinion toward North Korea. In April of the same year, KSM's headquarters hosted a dinner, inviting members from all sectors of society to reflect on the North Korean food crisis.[12]

About 700 people representing various vocational, religious, and social organ-izations, along with entrepreneurs and politicians, gathered for the dinner. The result was a public plea for nationwide participation in the campaign to help starving North Koreans.[13]

Since March 1997, this kind of public appeal has played a critical role in creating a favorable atmosphere for assisting North Korea, laying the foundation for broad public campaigns. Letters were sent to the media pleading for more assistance, and the *Hangyorae* newspaper responded positively. While the KSM played a pivotal role, hundreds of small groups also took part. The Kim Young Sam government could not block voluntary civilian movements, although it had been able to constrain aid activities undertaken by businesses and the media. In addition, the leaders of religious groups were part of the voluntary movement, over which governmental control was impossible. In a nutshell, the aid activities for North Korea were started by the collection of funds solicited by the "ant corps"—a relatively small group of representatives of grassroots organizations. Public figures outside the government who had been closely involved with the democratization process in the past joined the ant corps, as did organizations such as the Young Men's Christian Association (YMCA) and the progressive Korean Federation of Farmers and Korean Federation of Trade Unions. In all, roughly 4 million people joined the campaign, collecting about $4.5 million (4 billion won) in cash. This was the largest national campaign since the March 1 Independence Movement in 1919.[14]

The Kim Young Sam government was concerned about the growth of this campaign, so it sent official directives to schools to remind them that the ROK National Red Cross was the only channel for aid provision to North Korea. It launched investigations into some of the civilian organizations on charges of diverting collected funds, invoking regulations concerning the collection of donations that forbade collection costs to exceed 2 percent of the collected funds. Such scrutiny was designed to tarnish the moral character of the civilian organizations by subjecting them to spurious investigations by prosecutors.

The attitude of the North Korean regime also became a negative factor. For example, North Korea constructed the extravagant Kumsusan Memorial Palace to commemorate its late leader Kim Il Sung, diverting scarce resources that could have helped alleviate the suffering of its people. In Seoul, demonstrations by conservative anticommunist groups escalated. The demonstrators argued, "The food we sent to the North will return as bullets targeting us." This was the heart of the dilemma: North Korea's seemingly callous attitude toward its people has been the reason so many governments and NGOs have had difficulties with sending aid to the DPRK. It was one of the main reasons why the South Korean government felt obliged to take a passive stance on assisting suffering North Koreans. North Korea avoided government-level talks with South Korea and continued its provocations. Beyond the 1996 submarine incursion into the South, there were demonstrations on the Demarcation Line, a shooting incident on the west coast, talk of war as an option, and numerous military parades. The South Korean government responded by arguing that a reduction of only 5 percent in North Korea's defense budget could resolve the food crisis. The skepticism about North Korea was reinforced by wishful thinking about its possible collapse. [15]

LIMITATIONS OF THE SINGLE-CHANNEL POLICY

According to NGO workers, South Korean NGOs, including the Join Together Society (JTS), used China as an indirect channel to the North. And, as mentioned above, they also assisted the North through international NGOs. For instance, World Vision Korea (WVK) sent five tons of rice to North Korea via World Vision International. EBCF served as a channel for South Korean Christian NGOs engaged in aiding starving North Koreans. Some NGOs even ran cooperative farms (though on a small scale) in Chinese areas bordering North Korea to provide food directly to North Koreans. Most South Korean NGOs were closely linked to religious organizations.

Meanwhile, following a meeting of representatives from the Red Cross organizations of both South and North, Seoul and Pyongyang finally agreed that the South would directly provide 53,000 tons of corn collected by the private sector, instead of distributing it by way of the IFRC. The South and North also agreed to designated donations (that is, they would allow donations to be designated to particular places or agencies), opening a new chapter in cooperation. Nevertheless, the South Korean National Red Cross still remained the only official channel for assistance to North Korea.[16]

This single-channel policy caused several major problems. The first was the issue of monitoring, which was necessary to secure transparency in the distribution of food assistance. The food aid that went to North Korea via the South Korean National Red Cross was sent to Shinuiju, Nampo, and Namyang, each of which was monitored by only one IFRC official. In other words, food aid to North Korea gathered by South Korean civilian organizations had to be sent through the South Korean National Red Cross, so accurate monitoring depended on the monitoring capacity of the IFRC, which made the deliveries. Therefore, it could not be confirmed whether the food was appropriately distributed to North Korean residents. Moreover, most of the food assistance sent to North Korea via the South Korean National Red Cross was simply routed to the central government of North Korea. While some of the food aid had designated destinations by region, overall control of the food was in the hands of the central government. As a result, cases of food never reaching famine-stricken regions occurred frequently, leading to suspicions about food diversion for military use.[17]

EFFECT OF PLURAL CHANNELS AND EXPANDED EXCHANGES

Given that the provision of food aid via the South Korean National Red Cross had monitoring limitations, civilian organizations continued to demand multiple channels for assistance to North Korea. They asserted that more diverse exchanges and contacts were needed to lay the groundwork for national reconciliation through humanitarianism and ultimate unification. The year 1997 was a turning point for South Korean NGO pleas for domestic acceptance of North Korean aid, with large portions of the South Korean population overcoming their "Red menace" fears. The shift was in part a demonstration of the national confidence arising from a belief in the superiority of the South Korean political and economic system: North Koreans were no longer enemies to fight against but were now seen as brothers and sisters who must be saved from devastation. The idea of a national mission to free North Korea from famine gained support, as did the idea that South Korea should help the North onto the track of economic development. Unfortunately, however, the 1997 Asian financial crisis had a negative impact on this movement, dampening the mood of the South Korean people.

From 1995 until 2001, assistance to North Korea totaled more than $1.6 billion from all sources. Of that amount, approximately $591.96 million was donated by South Korea—$430.05 million from the government and $161.91 million from NGOs (see Appendices A, B, and C).[18]

When the more liberal Kim Dae Jung administration took office in 1998, South Korean NGOs finally had the opportunity to receive official recognition and support from the government, and relief efforts took on a greater variety of forms. For example, organizations including Good People, the International Corn Foundation (ICF), the National Coalition of NGOs for Inter-Korea Agricultural

Development and Cooperation, KSM, WVK, JTS, and Good Neighbors Korea (GNK) participated in cooperative projects to help North Korea.[19]

These organizations tried to help implement fundamental reforms in North Korean agricultural structure through a number of projects. These included the super corn growth project, contract growth of seed potatoes, assistance for sericulture, nurturing milk-producing goats through a pilot ranch assistance project, greenhouse construction, dairy development, and agricultural farming technology and material assistance.[20]

In addition, KWF, EBCF, Medical Aid for Children of the D.P.R.Korea Good Neighbors, WVK, and Okkedongmu Children in Korea (Friends Standing Shoulder to Shoulder) launched a variety of medical assistance projects, including provision of nutrition pills for children, medical supplies for pediatricians, tuberculosis eradication, provision of meals, parasite extermination, and the establishment of pharmaceutical companies. The movement toward development assistance and capacity-building projects as additions to emergency relief projects drew increasing interest. What was attractive about the cooperative agricultural reform projects was that the monitoring and access issues could be simultaneously resolved in a rather smooth manner, with the provision of farming implements, seeds, and agricultural technology.

THE SUNSHINE POLICY AND NGO ACTIVITIES

The launch of the Kim Dae Jung government, with its active engagement policy dubbed the "Sunshine Policy," opened a new chapter in humanitarian assistance for North Korea. First, the Kim Dae Jung administration allowed NGOs to visit North Korea to discuss assistance with North Korean officials as well as to monitor the relief process. Accordingly, in April 1998, KSM's co-president, Kang Mun-kyu, and its executive director, Soe Kyung-suk, visited North Korea to survey the food situation and discuss agricultural cooperation. The ROK government also expanded the opportunities for fundraising for North Korea, giving NGOs a freer hand in humanitarian activities.[21]

In September 1998, the South Korean government for the first time allowed some civilian organizations to directly supply North Korea with relief goods, letting them share the role with the South Korean National Red Cross, which had previously monopolized the aid channel to the North. In February 1999, the government finally approved a multiple-channel approach, opening more avenues for contact with North Korea and allowing civilian organizations to help North Korea independently. Civilian organizations had pointed out that the single channel of the South Korean National Red Cross inadvertently consolidated the central distribution system in the North.[22] In doing so, they argued, the single channel made it more difficult to induce North Korea to follow the path of reform and open up. The ROK government's insistence on the single Red Cross channel was designed to hide its concern about weakening the South Korean National Red Cross's negotiating power in dealings with its counterpart, the North Korean Red Cross.[23]

The South Korean government finally allowed the use of multiple channels in order to facilitate provision of modest assistance at the most appropriate time and also to acknowledge the NGOs' desire to make direct contact with North Korea. The change was expected to help achieve several goals, including increasing contacts between the North and South Korean people, facilitating inter-Korean exchanges and cooperation, and displaying the Seoul government's intention to pursue a forward-looking policy toward North Korea. From 1999 to 2000, 10 NGOs provided humanitarian assistance to North Korea on 52 occasions, amounting to, on average, help for the North once a week. Civilian organizations visited North Korea by land, air, and sea, using routes linking Beijing and Pyongyang, Inchon and Nampo, and Dandong and Shinuiju.[24]

South Korea legislated regulations on humanitarian relief work for North Korea during 2000 to promote the efficiency and relevance of projects, as well as to set appropriate standards for providing funds from the North-South Korea Cooperation Fund to the NGOs aiding North Korea.[25]

The amount of assistance to be provided was based on the aid projects' achievements in the previous year, the appropriateness of the projects and the recipients of the assistance, the degree of transparency of distribution, the track records of past projects that had received funds, the efficacy of projects, and the priority of the government policy. The Ministry of Unification would support the following projects: general relief for flood victims and restoration; agricultural projects to ease the food crisis; medical projects to improve health care, hygiene, and nourishment of children and the elderly; projects to restore vegetation, preventing natural disasters and protecting the environment; and other projects that the ministry deemed appropriate.[26]

Twenty-four organizations that would be engaged exclusively in assisting North Korea were set up through their own channels, actively operating primarily for emergency relief work and simple material supply, as well as other cooperative projects. In the process, the Ministry of Unification was authorized to support these organizations financially for the sake of North-South Korea exchanges and cooperation.

In addition to supporting an economic system based on the principle of separating business from politics, the ROK government actively supported South Korean companies' investment in North Korea. A case in point was the visit of Chung Ju-yung, honorary chairman of Hyundai, to North Korea with his "cattle diplomacy." The chairman visited North Korea with cattle herds as a gift and successfully opened a new tourism project on Mt. Kumgang. The Hyundai project, however, which pursued profits through economic cooperation for a west coast industrial complex, was a nonprofit, private sector project. The project was expected to increase civilian contacts, deepen economic dependency, and bring political benefits to the Seoul government. The government had high expectations that these projects pursued by Hyundai would facilitate inter-Korean economic cooperation more than anything else besides private sector aid to North Korea. Some South Korean conglomerates, however, cooperated with the government's North Korea policy merely as a bid to avert the government's aggressive demand for comprehensive reforms of their family-dominated *chaebol* system. For this purpose, they sent lavish gifts and cash to North Korean leader Kim Jong Il. [27]

In approving NGO projects in North Korea, the ROK government set certain standards: respect for the law, professionalism, and the capacity to ensure transparency of distribution. Based on the scale of assistance, each NGO opened and operated its own channel for dialogue with various counterparts in North Korea, including the APPC, Chosun Christian Alliance, National Reconciliation Council, Chosun Buddhist Alliance, North Korea Red Cross, Chosun Catholic Alliance, Friendship Society of Overseas Koreans, National Economic Association, and Najin-Sunbong Administrative Economic Committee.[28] The efficiency and professionalism of the assistance has been enhanced through contacts with each respective channel, while NGOs are making regular visits to North Korea, monitoring within a limited scope.

When the Kim Dae Jung administration proclaimed its Sunshine Policy in 1998, North Korean authorities regarded it as a more dangerous policy than the previous one—and one that would ultimately undermine the North Korean regime. [29] The DPRK regime worried about possible contamination from capitalism, cautioning against the "poisoned carrot." The so-called "mosquito net theory" was a demonstration of its willingness to accept outside assistance selectively, while preemptively averting damaging outside influence. In the initial stages, when South Korean NGOs launched aid projects for North Korea, the North Korean authorities suspected aid workers of being spies.[30]

In the meantime, some South Koreans criticized NGO projects as a communist plot designed to support the Kim Jong Il regime. Furthermore, North Korea had a system that was, and still is, fairly stable and resistant to change.[31] North Korea was in command even when receiving help from NGOs; sometimes it was cooperative and sometimes it refused to cooperate, citing "internal circumstances."

EFFECTS OF THE INTER-KOREAN SUMMIT

The inter-Korean summit between DPRK leader Kim Jong Il and ROK President Kim Dae Jung in June 2000 had a dramatic impact on nearly all aspects of North-South relations, including humanitarian aid efforts for the North. The summit increased South Korea's interest in nurturing a stable relationship with the North in the hopes of peaceful reconciliation and eventual reunification. As a result, humanitarian projects were enlarged dramatically as the government began to get involved.[32] Private companies, local governments, and schools expanded their participation in activities designed to assist in North Korea's rehabilitation. ROK governmental assistance increased from $11 million in 1998 to $28.25 million in 1999, and to $78.63 million in 2000.

Before the summit, President Kim Dae Jung in his Berlin Declaration offered expanding economic cooperation between the two Koreas.[33] For this he called on North Korea to accept four proposals—government-level cooperation, active response to overtures for reconciliation and cooperation, resolution of divided family issues, and acceptance of special envoy exchanges. The South Korean government also proposed to create a more favorable environment for private companies to invest in North Korea. It would do this by first improving infrastructure such as roads, ports, railroads, electricity, and telecommunications. Second, as part of solving the food crisis, an agreement would be reached on investment guarantees and avoidance of double taxation. Finally, agricultural reforms through fertilizer assistance, and improvements on farming equipment and irrigation systems would be made, again as part of solving the food crisis. These proposals recognized the need to induce inter-Korean economic cooperation in the private sector.[34]

The level of financial support from NGOs, which had been the major players in assisting the North, declined. North Korea seemed to be more interested in assistance from the South Korean government than from NGOs. The role of international NGOs in providing food and fertilizers significantly decreased following the inter-Korean summit, dropping from $358.7 million in 1999 to $106.07 million in 2000. Expanded governmental involvement further undercut the work of civilian organizations by increasing North Korea's expectations, which soon surpassed the civilian organizations' capacity to fulfill them. From a North Korean perspective, it was more advantageous to receive food and fertilizers from the South Korean government than from NGOs, for a variety of reasons. First, when aid from the South Korean government arrived at the Nampo port in the North, there was no monitoring by any international organization and no requirement to submit follow-up data detailing the distribution or use of the aid. Moreover, the amounts of aid were significant. Following the inter-Korean summit meeting, the ROK government became the North's major source of aid, providing loans that contributed significantly to easing the food crisis.[35]

The ROK government also dominated the dissemination of public information on assistance projects to North Korea. Consequently, the South came to assume more of a moral burden in demonstrating the intentions of the South vis-à-vis the North, and the NGOs' status and role were thus relatively weakened. This shift was in sharp contrast to the situation in the United States and the European Union, both of which continued to use NGOs to implement projects supported by aid from such semigovernmental agencies as the U.S. Agency for International Development (USAID) and the European Commission's Humanitarian Aid Office (ECHO).

In fact, on his visit to the North, President Kim Dae Jung included in his entourage figures from the government, private companies, and academia, but he inadvertently slighted the NGOs that had long been engaged in humanitarian projects in the North and failed to include any representatives of the opposition party. Moreover, in the wake of the summit talks, there were no discussions on ways to facilitate the activities of civilian aid organizations.[36]

MEASURES OF MINISTRY OF UNIFICATION HUMANITARIAN PROJECTS

Meanwhile, it became vitally important to fine-tune communication between NGOs and the South Korean government—especially between NGOs and the Ministry of Unification. In 2000, 26 NGOs organized a consultative body, composed of civil organizations for humanitarian assistance to North Korea, to enhance efficiency and facilitate exchanges of information and cooperation.[37] Chaired by WVK president Oh Jae-shik, these organizations made several requests of the government: to include figures from civilian groups in the North-South Exchanges Cooperation Promotion Committee; to institutionalize cooperation between the government and the private sector; to adopt matching funds for NGOs; to introduce non-interest-bearing loans; and to provide food and fertilizer via civilian organizations.[38] The idea of matching funds to assist North Korea was borrowed from the model of the Canadian Foodgrains Bank. Policy consultations between the Ministry of Unification and civilian groups commenced in 2001. Civilian members included the ICF, KSM, GNK, Good Friends, and KWF. Participating on the government's side were the Humanitarian Affairs Bureau of the Ministry of Unification; the Ministries of Agriculture, Welfare, Labor, and Environment; and experts from the Agricultural Community Economic Research Institute and the Korean Institute for National Unification.[39]

The Ministry of Unification provided matching funds to be used for projects by NGOs. In 2000 and 2001, KSM, WVK, EBCF, and ICF received funds amounting to about $7.7 million (10 billion won) from the North-South Korea Exchanges and Cooperation Fund. However, there was a cap on the provision of funds, and only projects lasting more than one year were eligible for the government's matching funds—a policy that dissatisfied the NGOs.[40]

The Ministry of Unification restricted its funding assistance to each organization to $770,000 (1 billion won). This amount could only be claimed by organizations that provided assistance in the range of 1.5 billion won. This caused some of the larger organizations to split up to get more government funds. On the other hand, some organizations that operated within a budget of 1.5 billion won opted not to involve themselves in projects exceeding the threshold amount. As a result, there were complaints among NGOs that the government matching funds were not helpful. Moreover, the Ministry of Unification would not accept a plan to commit necessary projects to NGOs. As cooperation between NGOs and the ROK government, as well as among NGOs themselves, remained nascent, there was inevitable competition for funds. The provision of matching funds by the Ministry of Unification for certain organizations deepened the competition among civilian organizations.[41]

However, the Ministry of Unification was legitimately concerned about inefficiencies arising from redundant or overlapping projects among civilian organizations and the imbalance arising from the increase in the number of South Korean NGOs while the number of North Korean counterparts was fixed.

Furthermore, it was important to increase transparency.[42] The growing tension created the need to facilitate policy consultation between the Ministry of Unification and humanitarian NGOs.

LAME-DUCK EFFECT OF THE SUNSHINE POLICY

The inter-Korean summit was a first, but its achievements did not represent a dramatic change in direction. In fact, in many respects it was the culmination of a process of inter-Korean contacts that had taken place over decades. Even the Park Chung Hee regime had gained symbolic positive results from engagement with North Korea at the height of the Cold War. However, as a result of the summit, President Kim did reframe government policy for the first time in a post–Cold War setting, emphasizing confidence-building and peaceful coexistence rather than confrontation as the fundamental premise of his policy.[43]

The Kim Dae Jung administration tried to accelerate the process of reconciliation and peaceful coexistence with North Korea. This inevitably made the Blue House the target of criticism from conservatives. Factors both within and outside South Korea did not strengthen President Kim's attempts to secure North-South reconciliation. When U.S. President George W. Bush took office in 2001, the change in command was accompanied by tougher rhetoric about North Korea, since the Bush administration was far less willing to engage North Korea than the Clinton administration had been. Pyongyang did not react well to the perceived and real slights from Washington, which provided cover for the North to put the brakes on an inter-Korean reconciliation process that had already slowed since November 2000. The South Korean public and media were quick to lay the blame exclusively on Washington for this slowdown in inter-Korean relations, even though the deceleration had begun before the U.S. presidential elections.

Domestic politics also had a significant impact on the ROK government's policy toward North Korea. Support for the Sunshine Policy plummeted, adversely affecting relief projects for North Korea. Aid from South Korea declined nominally in 2001 to $70.45 million as momentum in inter-Korean relations suddenly dissipated (see Appendix B). It was difficult to create bipartisan consensus, with the conservatives posing the greatest opposition. The lack of national consensus resulted from inept sharing of information and the ruling party's monopoly over the engagement process in the name of "sunshine." Moreover, North-South cooperative projects, such as civilian and cultural exchanges—which were another axis of inter-Korean exchanges linked to humanitarian assistance projects—faced hurdles in the wake of the August 2001 Grand National Unification Festival.

The clash in views between the conservatives and the radicals (frequently referred to as the South-South conflict) deepened, which in turn fanned skepticism about the Sunshine Policy toward the North. The conservatives asserted that Seoul was "giving too much to the North." Consequently, unification minister Lim Dong-won, Korea's version of Germany's Egon Bahr (who, in the 1970s, aggressively pursued Neue Ostpolitik to engage East Germany), resigned as a result of a no-confidence vote in the National Assembly in September 2001.

Since the engagement policy was inextricably interwoven with internal politics, it was sometimes exploited or restrained by domestic politics. The engagement of North Korea was portrayed as a personal glory for President Kim Dae Jung rather than a victory for the whole nation. Ironically, this perception was exacerbated domestically when Kim Dae Jung was named the recipient of the 2000 Nobel Peace Prize in October, only three months after his landmark visit to Pyongyang. The relationship between the South and North was also regarded as a one-sided love affair, lacking reciprocity and verifiability; as a result, it gradually lost public support. In the end, overly optimistic expectations for a durable peace with North Korea and euphoria at the prospect of ultimate unification fizzled out. Thus, the Kim Dae Jung administration could not help but depend on the North's positive response in order to ensure the success of the Sunshine Policy. By late 2002, some analysts even argued that Kim Jong Il felt he had been misled by grandiose promises of assistance laid out in the Berlin Declaration, promises that, in the end, Kim Dae Jung had failed to deliver. As internal political problems in the South heightened mistrust of the government, public support for the Sunshine Policy nose-dived, damaging support for continued dialogue and engagement with North Korea.

SOUTH KOREAN NGOS AND THEIR ACTIVITIES

As mentioned, the inter-Korean summit led the North to lean toward large-scale aid from the South Korean government, making the status of South Korean NGOs relatively weakened. In such an unfavorable situation, the NGOs quickened the pace of humanitarian activities in an effort to sustain the euphoric atmosphere on the Korean peninsula. This was in sharp contrast with western NGOs, which were showing signs of donor fatigue. South Korean NGOs tried to correct misunderstandings arising from the conservatives' Cold War mindset by informing this elite group of facts about North Korea based on the observations of NGO personnel during direct visits and interactions. Most South Korean NGOs involved with humanitarian assistance held a liberal nationalistic perspective that was quite different, of course, from the view of members of the conservative elite. [44]

This perspective was not prompted by fantasies about North Korea, but was instead a result of the simple reality that over the long term, there is no alternative to engagement. In addition, as the official inter-Korean relationship slowed, there was a reevaluation in Pyongyang of the importance of NGOs. [45]

Compared with the resources available from the South Korean government, the assistance provided by NGOs was on a small scale. But North Korea realized that the NGOs' role as a provider of assistance should not be underestimated. For the South Korean side, NGOs provided a consistency and "objectivity" that created a safety net for an engagement policy toward the North that could help buffer the fallout from domestic political debates.

In the new context of an improved relationship with Seoul and strong hostility from Washington, Pyongyang found it nearly impossible to return to old patterns; namely, using confrontation and tension to its own ends. Instead, Pyongyang seemed to be seeking an honorable, face-saving exit from this confrontational stance, as well as more support and benefits—not only from South Korea but also from the international community. To that end, Pyongyang wanted to take advantage of the activities of the South Korean NGOs.

FOOD AID AND AGRICULTURAL COOPERATION

The devastation caused by the famine in North Korea was not a natural but a man-made disaster.[46] The innate structural distortions in North Korean agriculture were simply aggravated by the natural disasters of the mid-1990s.[47] Massive emergency food relief was provided by such international organizations as the WFP and IFRC. The South Korean government joined in the distribution of similarly massive supplies of both food and fertilizer. No fundamental solutions to the country's structural problems in agriculture were applied, however. Relatively speaking, South Korean NGOs took a smaller role in food provision during the crisis.[48] Since 2000, the South Korean government's massive food aid to the North has continued in full swing, while interest in food aid by civil organizations has declined.

Food aid from the international community dropped from $226.3 million in 1999 to $106.66 million in 2000, a decline of nearly 70 percent. In 2001, the Seoul government provided 100,000 tons of corn to North Korea through the WFP, along with 200,000 tons of fertilizer.[49]

South Korean NGOs argued that providing aid to North Korea via NGOs rather than via the government was more efficient than going through the WFP. By giving NGOs the primary responsibility, they emphasized, civilian exchanges furthering inter-Korean reconciliation could be facilitated. In addition, they argued, NGOs would conduct monitoring more effectively and, with increased knowledge, could expand their participation into other fields of assistance. The South Korean government, however, preferred massive direct aid shipments—a stance that inevitably weakened the status of South Korea's NGOs by limiting them to relatively small-scale humanitarian activities. Timely NGO provision of even a small amount of aid became more difficult, eventually minimizing the window of opportunity for cooperation between the government and civil organizations.

Some South Korean NGOs refute allegations of possible diversion of food aid donations to North Korea's military.[50] They point out that 200,000–300,000 tons of food a year are required to feed 1 million soldiers of the Korean People's Army. If the average domestic grain production in the North amounts to at least 2 million tons a year, the issue of food hoarding for the military is of little concern. Furthermore, these NGOs point out, there are strict control mechanisms in place: If a soldier is caught stealing food, he is put to death by firing squad. Thus, they argue, there is only a remote possibility of diversion of food to the military.

South Korean NGOs run cooperative projects in conjunction with general relief efforts. NGOs have increasingly been requested to assist North Korea in restructuring its agricultural system, in addition to providing emergency relief aid. Thus, agricultural cooperation is the core practical project through which to improve inter-Korean relations. This type of project has gained support, because visits to certain regions on a regular and continuing basis improve the monitoring process and provide technical training, as well as increasing private contacts. NGOs are therefore focusing on providing support for North Korea to improve its agricultural productivity, despite North Korea's insistence on "assistance before cooperation." Thus, NGOs have found that they need to pursue emergency relief efforts and general relief work simultaneously. For instance, while moving ahead with cooperative projects in agriculture, the KSM is providing vitamin-enriched bread, WVK is sending flour and powdered milk, and GNK is delivering powdered milk, nutritional meals, clothing, and daily necessities.

Showing their dissatisfaction with North Korea's insistence on "relief before cooperation," western NGOs have made it clear that they will no longer fund regions they cannot enter.[51] Under these circumstances, it may be possible for South Korean NGOs to expand their activities in the North. The first case of agricultural cooperation between South and North Korea, led by a South Korean NGO, was the agricultural cooperative in Durae village in the North; the cooperative is now being promoted by six specialized assistance organizations, including the ICF, KSM, WVK, the National Coalition of NGOs for Inter-Korean Agricultural Development and Cooperation, Korea JTS, and GNK.[52]

During the initial stage, when these organizations provided agricultural implements, they did so with difficulty, with lack of cooperation among NGOs and lack of preparation for the work being the major obstacles. The most serious impediment to agricultural cooperation, however, was North Korea's insistence on following agricultural methods dictated by the *juche* (extreme self-reliance) ideology, which is directly linked to regime survival. The reluctance to admit lack of self-sufficiency is one of the main reasons why it has been difficult for North Korea to launch comprehensive structural reforms to resolve its fundamental problems.[53]

NGOs have attempted joint projects with North Korea for some years. However, the projects' small scale and the lack of information about the North Korean agricultural system have led to failure. South Korean NGOs have also tried to achieve modest success in small-scale assistance and cooperative projects on a gradual basis, despite the lack of information about North Korea and the unreliable and inadequate transportation system. For effective and continuous cooperative projects, there should be increased visits to North Korea by trained agricultural personnel.[54] The complicated process of invitations, social aversion to cooperative projects, and the difficulty of balancing supply and demand have emerged as stumbling blocks. In addition, securing monitoring and access and the need for greater professionalism in the agricultural sector have also presented challenges to successful implementation of this work.

The KSM started to promote contacts with the APPC of North Korea in early 1998. KSM members Seo Kyung-suk and Kang Mun-kyu visited North Korea in April 1998 for a survey of the North Korean food crisis and discussion of agricultural cooperative projects. At present, KSM is running agricultural cooperative projects that include the cultivation of potatoes, initiatives to increase sericulture productivity, and pilot ranch projects. It is assisting five cooperative farms—in Pyongyang, North and South Pyongan provinces, and North and South Hwanghae provinces—with production of major grain crops. It is also a liaison to the Academy of Agricultural Science of North Korea and its four branch offices. The sericulture project is operating in two counties in Jagang province in the northern part of the country. This is a high value-added project, attracting Kim Jong Il's special interest. When sericulture is well established in North Korea, the country will be able to produce silk cocoons and thread, while South Korea can specialize in silk production to take advantage of a division of labor between the two Koreas. A pilot ranch project involving milk-producing goats was designed to provide nutrition for North Korean infants, children, and pregnant women—the most vulnerable citizens during the prolonged food crisis. A pilot ranch was set up in the city of Pyongyang with the introduction of a herd of 450 milk-producing goats from New Zealand. KSM also provided milking and processing facilities.[55]

In 1998, GNK secured a contract with the General Administration Bureau of the National Ranch Management of the Agricultural Committee of North Korea, providing a herd of 200 dairy cows to a ranch that the NGO also operated. It also undertook the distribution of milk to children. In conjunction with the dairy cow project, GNK is also providing fodder, milking equipment, milk-pasteurizing pots, cream separators, and dairy cow semen. Grain fodder, essential for the growth of cows, is also being supplied. The number of cows is expected to increase from 200 to roughly 1,500 by 2003.[56]

GNK and the ICF have signed a contract with North Korea's Academy of Agricultural Science on inter-Korean agricultural technology cooperation and have pursued a joint research project to grow "super corn" in North Korea, along with a nationwide project to plant corn. The North Korean authorities gave special status to ICF president Kim Sun-kwon, allowing him to travel around North Korea with relative freedom. The ICF was established in 1998 and has maintained a relationship with the Academy of Agricultural Science of North Korea. Corn seeds developed in South Korea were provided to about 1,500 collective farms in North Korea, with the Hwanghae region receiving most of the assistance. There are no permanent representatives of the ICF in North Korea, but monitoring is being conducted during regular visits by ICF staff. An important project run by the ICF is to give advice to the Academy of Agricultural Science, which conducted a precision test in 10 test sites in North Korea to select the 30 most suitable seeds for development and growth. The nationwide corn-planting campaign is to provide a corn seed, known as Suwon 19, along with fertilizers and farming implements. In the years to come, it is also expected that a new seed suitable for North Korean soil conditions will be developed. In 1998,

5.2 tons of Suwon 19 were provided to 83 North Korean villages. In 1999, 39.5 tons of Suwon 19 were planted in 1,000 villages. It is interesting to note that an increase in the harvest was reported, compared with the harvest realized from North Korea's own seed type, Hwasung 1. In 2000, the ICF contract with North Korea was extended to 2007, and a specific agreement was reached on the corn-seed development project for research purposes. Meanwhile, ICF officials report that they are having difficulty developing super corn varieties because of the different social system and security constraints. For example, they have access to only 10 of 22 pilot research centers.[57]

WVK has succeeded in establishing a major project in North Korea to provide more effective methods of propagating seed potatoes.[58] WVK is the branch office of WVI and is engaged in one of the largest aid projects in North Korea.[59] Its North Korean contact point is the APPC. At the end of 1994, Koreans living in the United States released a report regarding the food situation in North Korea. On that basis, WVK provided food for Pyongyang and Hwanghae province. It built six noodle factories and then expanded its assistance to the agricultural and medical sectors. Through the seed potato project, WVK provided the materials needed for the construction of 3,300 square meters of greenhouses for water growth. Five North Korean agricultural experts were sent to Australia for training in connection with this project. In June 1999, cucumbers and tomatoes were harvested. The seed potato and noodle factory projects are middle- to long-term projects for WVK. In spring 2000, WVK, in cooperation with the Academy of Agricultural Science, started growing potato seeds that have now been planted in four regions—Hamgheung, Daeheungdan, Jungju, and Baechun—spreading the risk to reduce the possibility of failure. WVK optimistically predicts that 4 to 5 million tons of seed potatoes will be produced by the end of 2003.[60]

In October 1998, North Korean leader Kim Jong Il made an onsite visit to Daeheungdan county, the largest potato-producing region in North Korea, where he displayed great interest in the revolution in potato growing.[61] Potatoes grow well in the highlands, where they have an advantage over other agricultural products. The North Korean Ministry of Agriculture has doubled potato-growing areas and is planning further expansion in 2002. The National Coalition of NGOs for Inter-Korean Agricultural Development and Cooperation has also participated in the assistance project for potato production. Onsung county, Yanggang province, and Daeheungdan county in North Korea received 150 tons of seed potatoes, as well as fertilizers and agricultural chemicals.[62] Korea JTS improved agricultural techniques and successfully grew a small number of potatoes on a test basis. It also helped increase the production of corn and rice by three to five times by providing fertilizers and introducing new agricultural techniques. Korea JTS has constructed a nutritional food factory in the Najin-Sunbong region and has also helped build a cooperative farm there. Ethnic Koreans residing in China near the border were hired to carry out monitoring and other related activities. To show flexibility, JTS did not designate special recipients for the products of these projects.

MEDICAL ASSISTANCE AND PROTECTION
OF VULNERABLE GROUPS

When South Korean NGOs made their first visits to North Korea in the late 1990s to explore humanitarian cooperation in the medical field, North Koreans reacted negatively. A North Korean official demanded that South Korea should "Help those who are still alive. Never mind those who are sick and dying," a statement that puzzled visiting South Korean relief workers.[63]

The origins of medical assistance for North Korea can be traced back to the activities in the early 1990s of the U.S.-based Christian Association Medical Mission (CAMM), comprising Korean doctors living in the United States.[64] CAMM helped establish the Third People's Hospital in Pyongyang. When it faced difficulty with fundraising, however, the U.S. doctors' group asked for help from South Korean Christian groups. As free movement became possible in the Najin-Sunbong area following reform plans and the opening up of the region, the door to medical assistance also opened wide. The North America Christian Doctors Association, the Korean Welfare Foundation, and APPC chairman Kim Jung-woo played a central role in actualizing this assistance in the healthcare and medical areas.

Medical assistance projects, however, have not reached a satisfactory stage, even though there has been remarkable growth in the field, as evidenced by the increase in assistance from $1.6 million in 1997 to $12 million in 2000. Factors contributing to this growth have included North Korea's very evident need for medical assistance, as well as the enthusiasm of South Korean NGOs. The attraction of projects in this area was that these projects would promote cooperation without injuring the North Korean regime's pride. In contrast with agricultural cooperation efforts, North Korea did not have to worry about the infringement of *juche* ideology by getting medical assistance from the South. The focus of medical assistance projects has been on resolving fundamental long-term problems. Various projects have also been designed to meet the immediate needs of vulnerable groups, such as children and orphans.[65]

From 1995 to 2000, $9.7 million was used for medical material assistance. In 1995, medical assistance was mainly to prevent cholera and typhoid fever and to provide materials to be used for the construction of a new hospital. Participating organizations included Medical Aid for Children of the D.P.R.Korea, the Korean Welfare Foundation, Okkedongmu, and the EBCF.[66] Today, the KSM's health care and medical cooperation branch is leading a nationwide campaign, too. This is an encouraging sign, considering that there are only modest activities by international organizations in the health care and medical sector and that the international community's interest and support are decreasing.[67]

In fact, the health care and medical sector provides an opportunity for expanded cooperation because technical cooperation is relatively immune from political or ideological considerations. Contact points in North Korea are diverse. They include the Ministry of Public Health (Chosun Medical Association);

Pyongyang Medical College; Pyongyang Maternity Center; North Pyongan Children's Hospital; the Medical Committee for Overseas Koreans; People's Hospital in Pyongyang city, Gaechun city, and Sunbong county; and the Children's Nutrition Management Research Institute.[68] All express keen interest in improving and upgrading the regional medical system. As a socialist country, North Korea has had relatively well-equipped medical centers and a highly developed prevention mechanism. Unfortunately, however, the economic devastation of the past decade has led to the collapse of North Korea's medical system.[69] While medical facilities have remained, their operation and management capacity have been nonfunctional.[70]

Although North Korea maintains that its medical system is based on prevention, the system is not working because of equipment shortages and a lack of management capacity. Hospital meals for patients are also lacking—family members or friends must bring meals in. Efforts are being made to address the shortage of medical supplies by using traditional medicine and medicinal herbs. Herbs are replacing 70 percent of medical supplies. This shows that the lack of modern medicines is a far more serious problem than the lack of medical facilities.[71]

The KWF, established in 1996, reached a cooperative agreement with the DPRK to modernize Sunbong Hospital. In 1998, it also agreed to build a Rajin-Rodem pharmaceutical factory in conjunction with the Committee for the Promotion of External Economic Cooperation.[72] In the case of the Sunbong region, there were more than 100 doctors, but stethoscopes and other medical equipment or devices were a rarity. The North Korean counterpart was so sensitive about the Rajin-Rodem pharmaceutical factory project that it sometimes mobilized political propaganda, arguing that all the KWF-provided medical equipment labeled "made in Korea" was in fact made either in the United States or Japan. They even made a scene over the contents of the draft speech to be delivered at the groundbreaking ceremony for the factory. A gradual change is becoming evident, however, in the implementation of medical cooperation projects. In the initial stages, the National Security Agency's supervision and restrictions were frequent during the consultations about the provision of medical equipment. As time passed, however, supervision and restrictions were eased. Now, the agency is just acting as a "guide," according to testimony by relief workers. Setting aside its pride, it is quick to plead for more assistance, saying, "We need your help." This is the outcome of medical professionalism, mutual trust, and the North's desperate situation.

At the request of North Korea's Ministry of Health Care, medical projects have been conducted in Pyongyang and Shinuiju since 2000.[73] In 1997, the KWF offered five kinds of essential medicine (including children's vitamins and intestinal-worm pills) in its first official shipment of South Korean medicine to North Korea.[74] Since 1999, the major recipients of medical assistance have been children, and the modernization of pediatric hospitals, establishment of children's heart disease centers, meal distribution, antiparasite medicine assistance, and operation of pharmaceutical factories have taken place. Over the next five years, children under the age of 15 will be treated as part of a parasite extermination project. Considering the poor nutritional condition of North Korean children, Shinpoong Pharmaceutical Company of South Korea, the key provider of parasite extermination medicine, diluted the pills the children will take. The diluted pills were tested on the children of APPC staff members with positive results.[75]

As North Korea has gradually emerged from its isolation, increasing interest has been shown in ensuring the survival and development of vulnerable members of society. As admitted by North Korea's Ministry of Foreign Affairs, famine coupled with economic collapse has reduced the life expectancy of the 22 million North Koreans by more than six years. The death rate of children under age five increased from 27 to 48 per 1,000 between 1995 and 2001, while the infant mortality rate increased from 14 to 23 per 1,000. Between 1996 and 1998, the per capita GNP was cut nearly in half, plummeting from $991 to $457.

The protracted economic decline was, and still is, adversely affecting the electricity supply, efforts to prevent epidemics, and the water supply. Unstable electricity and inadequate water supply facilities are threatening children's health care.[76] NGOs are therefore focusing on children, to avoid the possibility of diversion of food aid to the military.

Medical Aid for Children of the D.P.R.Korea has provided medicine for children since 1997. The organization is composed of doctors, pharmacists, practitioners of Eastern medicine, and health care experts. It has provided medical goods and medicine such as vitamins, glucose, and amino acid for the DPRK Medical Society of the Ministry of Public Health. WVK is assisting the Children's Hospital of the Gaechun People's Hospital in Gaechun, South Pyongan province, providing basic medicine, medical equipment, blankets, and a noodle factory.[77]

EBCF made contact with the Flood Damage Rehabilitation Committee (FDRC) to participate in efforts to eradicate tuberculosis by providing medicine and nutrition supplements. Among foreigners, EBCF's founder, Dr. Stephen Linton, has the closest contacts with North Korea. In 1995, when North Korea appealed to the international community for help, it specifically named Dr. Linton.[78]

EBCF began assistance projects in 1996 and has been helping patients by administering the Directly Observed Treatment System (DOTS), the most advanced cure for tuberculosis. It also provides general relief items such as rice, corn, fertilizers, cultivators, and devices for greenhouse growth of vegetables during wintertime—together worth $10.5 million—in addition to assistance in the health care sector. The foundation also runs a program providing X-ray diagnosis vehicles, special medical equipment, and doctors' training programs for 13 tuberculosis hospitals at the county level.

Future EBCF projects include the provision of vitamins for children, antibiotics, skin care ointment, and medical equipment, as well as establishment of pharmaceutical factories, the eradication of diseases, and nutritional meals for children.[79] North Korean officials with whom the foundation is in contact are actively responding to the programs. As a civilian organization, however, EBCF still lacks the financial resources to meet North Korea's requests in various fields.

Continuing challenges for South Korean NGOs engaged in the health care sector include the need to establish broader cooperation with their North Korean counterparts while avoiding excessive competition and overlapping projects. It is necessary to develop projects that can reach North Koreans as direct recipients while also responding to the diverse views and expectations of their North Korean counterparts, including the Ministry of Public Health. Furthermore, the South's NGOs need to pursue projects suitable for the North Korean health care environment while avoiding diverting resources to temporary assistance. The most urgent need is to establish a comprehensive management and assistance system, including diagnosis, prescriptions, and preventive treatments. In other words, the highest priority is to find ways to help North Korea establish a basis on which it can deal with its own problems.

POINTS OF CONTACT

The North Korean APPC is the primary interface with South Korean NGOs. Depending on the type of project, the APPC conducts policy analyses and mobilizes workers from relevant executive agencies in support of NGO projects. The APPC falls under the control of the DPRK central committee of the Korean Workers' Party. It is exclusively responsible for dealing with South Korean affairs. Officially, it is in charge of civilian exchanges, but in actuality it serves more broadly as a vehicle for countries in the Asia-Pacific region seeking contact with North Korea in the absence of diplomatic relations. Overall, the APPC has greater clout than any other organization. It is widely known that the same positions in the APPC are higher than those in other organizations.[80]

Chun Kum-jin, who participated in the vice-ministerial talks in Beijing in 1998, was the APPC's deputy chairman. Chun also participated in talks between the governments of North and South Korea as a cabinet member. Kim Young-sun is the current APPC chairman and vice chairman of the DPRK's Committee for the Peaceful Unification of the Fatherland (PUF), a core organization of the Korean Workers' Party. The PUF is the supporting agency in charge of operations, while the APPC plays a more public role. APPC was used for the historic inter-Korean summit in June 2001. At the summit, a channel of communication was established between Kim Young-sun and Lim Dong-won, then National Intelligence Service (NIS) chief, as well as another channel between the APPC's Song Ho-kyong and then-minister of culture and tourism Park Ji-won, the latter being the closest associate to President Kim Dae Jung. The groundwork for these historic summit talks was prepared through these lines of communication.

The APPC has dealt with Hyundai and Daewoo since 1997 as part of the North's effort to earn foreign currency. It sometimes negotiated with South Korea's government exclusively and sometimes dealt with the government and NGOs simultaneously.

Until 2001, when the APPC withdrew from Beijing for unknown reasons, the KSM and other South Korean civilian organizations had contacted North Korea through the APPC branch in Beijing. Under this arrangement, the APPC and the NGOs had signed project agreements annually. In accordance with these agreements, a responsible North Korean agency designated by the APPC had conducted projects with South Korean NGO counterparts. NGOs contacted the Ministries of Agriculture and Public Health, along with other government organizations and lower-level workers, as executive branch organizations related to APPC. NGOs monitored deliveries under the control of specific agencies. For this purpose, NGOs generally made 15 visits to North Korea each year. North Korean officials are keenly aware of domestic politics and internal trends in South Korea. However, they avoid making personal comments on these matters and act according to direction from above. These officials are replaced at regular intervals to prevent the development of personal or unofficial relationships with South Korean NGOs. They speak English, and many of them have studied in Eastern Europe.

In contrast, South Korean NGOs have no access to information about their North Korean points of contact at the project level. Even though agents of South Korean NGOs have some information about their North Korean project personnel, it is difficult for them to reveal the information publicly. In some cases, they are even reluctant to disclose the identities of these points of contact.

Nevertheless, it is important for South Korean NGOs to maintain unofficial relations with their North Korean points of contact, at least to some degree, to enhance project efficiency and deepen private exchanges. In particular, aid workers from South Korean NGOs are well positioned to cultivate such exchanges, since—unlike workers from other international NGOs—they speak the same language and share a common history and culture with North Koreans. In this regard, the function of South Korean NGOs is significant in that it enlarges the scope of the humanitarian projects through increased exchanges at the lower levels of the North Korean regime, even though the exchanges rarely touch the upper echelons that wield decision-making power.

Civilian organizations are well aware that North Korea's political structure normally relies on oral rather than written agreements. They believe that if they insist upon a written agreement, it could lead to misunderstandings with the North Korean side. South Korean aid organizations can neither establish a permanent presence in North Korea nor monitor a site without prior notification. They have little contact with ordinary North Korean residents. Nevertheless, the NGOs argue that they are staying in North Korea on a permanent basis because they are able to make such frequent visits. Exchanges and cooperation at a lower level between South Korean NGOs and working-level officials from the North Korean government can be exercised. And yet, Pyongyang's rhetoric remains political and exclusive. Higher officials maintain that they receive relief aid from the international community, including South Korean NGOs, simply because the outside world is eager to provide it.[81] Face-saving matters. In fact, the North Korean authorities are not interested in laying the groundwork for greater cooperation and eventual unification. Their highest priority is regime survival.

THE DPRK'S RELIANCE ON *JUCHE*

South Korean NGOs express cautious optimism about the development of transparency, consistency, and accountability in North Korea. They believe that it is important to build trust, whether at lower or higher levels. Drawing from their experience, they believe that once mutual trust is established, it will be much easier to visit North Korea to carry out aid projects, enhance transparency, and improve accountability and verification. However, it will take time and patience to make North Korean authorities ultimately accept information-collection and monitoring procedures in their country. For example, when WVK implemented its project for seed potatoes and the ICF conducted its super-corn and other agricultural reform projects in North Korea, these organizations placed priority on confidence-building with the North Korean side. As the APPC was overwhelmed by the work that followed the June 2001 summit, there was a reduction in exchanges and contacts, and delays in some of the major projects. APPC, however, did delegate the continuation of some projects to the National Economic Cooperation Federation, including the Kwangmyung Trading Group.[82]

Meanwhile, the North's National Economic Federation and the National Reconciliation Council have also been making contact with South Korean organizations—although the two organizations rarely coordinate with one another. There are no horizontal policy consultations between them, only vertical orders from the central party. Therefore, decision making takes much longer than it would if the two organizations were to work in tandem.

South Korean NGOs are focused on respecting North Korea's pride and sovereignty in the processes of contacts and negotiations, recognizing that culture and value systems are important variables. Western relief agencies, on the other hand, have tended to dismiss these factors and therefore have experienced many more ups and downs as they have implemented their aid projects in North Korea.[83]

South Korean NGOs are more understanding of North Korea's rigidity, recognizing that it takes time and patience to lead North Koreans to open their minds. South Korean NGOs believe that the North Korean attitude has gradually changed, that mutual trust has begun to grow, and that North Korea is gradually overcoming its fear of systemic collapse. North Korea has cautiously let NGOs expand the content and geographical scope of relief activity and maintain continuing contacts. Admittedly, however, North Korea has not changed sufficiently to allow aid workers to do their jobs without excessive and prohibitive restrictions.

There are still various pending problems, such as the issue of North Korean defectors. For example, Good Friends (Center for Peace, Human Rights, and Refugees), successor to the Korean Buddhist Sharing Movement established in 1996, has undertaken the dangerous task of helping Korean defectors living in China. This NGO claims, however, that the thaw in inter-Korean relations following the summit talks has negatively affected its activities. Logically, in the wake of the summit, the South Korean government has tried to avoid any issues that might irritate North Korea.

NGO PERCEPTIONS OF NORTH KOREA

Although the diplomatic isolation of North Korea resulting from the end of the Cold War accelerated the country's economic crunch, the general crisis in the economy and society did not result in the collapse of the North Korean system. From the perspective of modern history, North Korea was trapped in a political regime marked by dynasties, colonial rule, and one-man dictatorship, with no experience in developing a civil society. There were no factions in the military, thus excluding the possibility of a military coup. The unique characteristics of inter-Korean relations in the post–Cold War era prevented exchanges on the Korean Peninsula. Therefore, the exchanges that took place at a private level in response to the devastating floods of 1995 were landmark events in the Korean Peninsula's modern history. North Korea was highly cautious with regard to South Korean NGOs, because it was not confident in its economic and political system. However, South Korean NGOs were not powerful enough to play a significant role in adjusting the relationship between the authorities of the two Koreas. They have, however, served as a buffer, playing a complementary role in the reduction of tensions between the two states. Gradually, they are penetrating North Korean society, helping to lead its government in the direction of change.

CONCLUSION

Until relatively recently, the strained nature of inter-Korean relations had blocked all avenues for exchange and cooperation for a half century. The Cold War, the division of the nation, and the dynamics of internal politics created a complicated paradigm—the only country in the world that does not have direct means for phone calls or other forms of communication with North Korea is South Korea. Only five years ago, it was unimaginable for ordinary South Koreans to enter North Korea. Since then, however, the environment has changed, with a number of South Koreans increasing their inter-Korean contacts and exchanges.

From the perspective of western NGOs, information sharing, contacts, and cooperation for monitoring in North Korea were unsatisfactory compared with their experiences in other countries. From South Korea's viewpoint, however, the mere fact that they were building trust with North Korean working-level officials, even if they had yet to gain regular access to ordinary citizens, was a landmark development in itself—which indicates just how impenetrable the barrier between North and South Korea had grown over the years. Moreover, dissatisfied with the self-imposed isolation of Pyongyang, many western aid organizations withdrew from North Korea. Interest in providing aid to North Korea was also declining as a result of shifts in the international political situation. In addition, the cooling-off period in inter-Korean relations, along with the strained relations between North Korea and the United States, increased possibilities for more robust activities by South Korean organizations. Still, the problem of securing financial resources has not yet been satisfactorily resolved.

While South Korean NGOs are largely constrained by the circumstances governing inter-Korean relations, at the same time they have contributed to lowering existing tensions between the two Koreas. For example, amidst the rising tensions between North and South Korea sparked by the naval clashes in the West (Yellow) Sea in June 1999 and 2002, NGOs continued to visit and manage their projects in North Korea. In this circumstance, however, North Korea might have taken advantage of South Korean NGOs to test the South Korean government's will to engage the North.

For long-term peaceful management of a divided Korean Peninsula and in the interest of ultimate unification, the government, private enterprise, and NGOs should play complementary roles. Ideally, the engagement of North Korea through economic cooperation and humanitarian aid projects should create a synergistic effect.[84]

For this to happen, it is necessary to induce North Korea to open wider the channels of communication and contact. Closer linking between people of the North and South can open more opportunities for exchanges and cooperation. When there are expanded contacts between the two sides, professional projects can be undertaken and successfully completed. Also, by placing greater emphasis on the agencies in charge of implementing projects in each sector, it will be possible to block interference from higher up. North Korea has revealed its inefficiency by sometimes contacting more than one international organization to request redundant assistance. Yet it failed to allow free passage and access to the vulnerable groups for medical treatment and monitoring, which are essential for relief work. [85]

In sum, aid projects carried out by South Korean NGOs have not been powerful enough to induce North Korea to change dramatically. In spite of this, however, after seven years of aid work in North Korea, the NGOs are witnessing small but significant changes taking place in North Korea. While the South Korean government focuses on the DPRK leadership, the civilian organizations focus on the ordinary people. South Korea's NGOs pursue ambitious and idealistic goals in their aid efforts—more so than the government—and concentrate on lessening the North Korean people's sufferings. Ultimately, the hope is that the humanitarian assistance delivered by South Korean NGOs is playing an indirect role in achieving the grand cause of bringing stability and peace to the Korean Peninsula. Thus far, South Korean NGOs can at least take comfort from the perception that they have helped to address North Korea's internal crises in ways that have brought aid to long-lost brothers and sisters, who otherwise might not have received any help at all.

NOTES

1. Lee Yong-sun, interview by Chung Oknim, January 2002.
2. Steve Glain, "Defector Claims North Korea Has Five Bombs," *The Wall Street Journal,* 28 July 1994; Chung Oknim, *The 588 Days of the North Korean Nuclear Crisis* (in Korean), (Seoul: Seoul Press, 1995), p. 227.

3. A prior decision by the Japanese government to supply food assistance to the DPRK helped spur the South Korean government's decision to offer assistance.

4. Lee Kum-sun, "Ways to Improve Humanitarian Aid to North Korea; Focusing on Development Relief" (in Korean), *Research Collection 2000-32* (Seoul: Unification Research Institute), p. 7.

5. Lee Kum-sun, "Assessment and Prospects for Humanitarian Aid to North Korea," paper prepared for the Third International NGO Conference on Humanitarian Assistance to North Korea: Cooperative Efforts Beyond Food Aid, Yongin, South Korea, 17–20 June 2001.

6. Lee Jong-moo, "Humanitarian Assistance toward North Korea in South Korea: Historical and Current Overview for the South Korean Context," paper presented at the Third International NGO Conference on Humanitarian Assistance to North Korea: Cooperative Efforts Beyond Food Aid, Yongin, South Korea, 17–20 June 2001.

7. Lee Kum-sun, "Assessments and Prospects," p. 9, note 4.

8. *Korean Sharing Movement: Materials for Five Years of Activities since Establishment* (in Korean), (Seoul: Korean Sharing Movement, 2002).

9. A total of roughly $190,000 (170 million won) was collected in donations by the Korean Buddhist Chogye Order, Roman Catholic Archdiocese of Seoul, Council of Buddhist Orders, and Chondoist Central Headquarters.

10. Jae Sung-ho, "Ways to Improve Laws to Stimulate Civilian Assistance to North Korea," in *Korean Sharing Movement: Materials for the Five Years of Activities since Establishment* (in Korean), (Seoul: Korean Sharing Movement, 2002), p. 119.

11. Lee Kum-sun, "Assessments and Prospects," p. 12, note 4.

12. Secretary General Lee Yong-sun, interview, Korean Sharing Movement, 18 January 2002.

13. *Korean Sharing Movement: Materials for the Five Years of Activities since Establishment* (in Korean), (Seoul: Korean Sharing Movement, 2002), p. 10. Bishop Kim Su-han, Reverend Kang Won-yong, and KSM Executive Director Soe Yong-hun played major roles.

14. Soe Kyung-suk, "Directions for Civilian Cooperation between South Korea and Japan for Humanitarian Assistance to North Korea"(report in Korean), (Seoul: Korean Sharing Movement, 2002), p. 130.

15. Soe Kyung-suk, "Current Status of Inter-Korean Civilian Exchanges and Ways to Stimulate Them" (report in Korean), (Seoul: Korean Sharing Movement, 2002), p. 101.

16. Lee Jong-moo, interview, Korean Sharing Movement, January 2001.

17. Choi Chang-mu, "Tasks for Helping the North Korean People"(in Korean), in *Korean Sharing Movement: Materials for the Five Years of Activities since Establishment* (Seoul: Korean Sharing Movement, 2002).

18. Organizing Committee of the International NGO Conference on Cooperation with North Korea, Materials for the Third International NGO Conference on Humanitarian Assistance to North Korea: Cooperative Efforts Beyond Food Aid, Yongin, South Korea, 17–20 June 2001.

19. In the past, aid was oriented toward emergency relief, but now it began to shift toward agricultural restoration and focusing assistance on vulnerable groups and the health care sector. Ven Pomnyun, "Present Conditions and Future Questions of Food and Other General Relief Work," paper presented at the Third International NGO Conference on Humanitarian Assistance to North Korea: Cooperative Efforts Beyond Food Aid, Yongin, South Korea, 17–20 June 2001.

20. Kim Sun-kwon, "Current Status and Tasks for Agricultural Assistance" (in Korean), paper presented at the Third International NGO Conference on Humanitarian Assistance to North Korea: Cooperative Efforts Beyond Food Aid, Yongin, South Korea, 17–20 June 2001.

21. The government sought practical ways to focus on agricultural structural reforms, exchanges, and contacts with the North Korean people beyond emergency relief. Regulations on donation collection for North Korea were significantly eased, allowing a

variety of collection events. On the basis of the judgment that the North Korean food crisis was a man-made one rather than a natural disaster, the government recognized the need to come up with plans to support children and the elderly, and to restore and develop North Korea. Ministry of Unification, "Plans on Activating NGO Humanitarian Activities for the DPRK," 16 March 1998.

22. Interview by the author with an NGO worker, June 2001.

23. Lee Kum-sun, "Ways to Improve Humanitarian Aid," p. 19, note 4.

24. Lee Jong-moo, "Current Status of Agricultural Cooperation between Civilian Organizations and North Korea," (report in Korean), (Seoul: Korean Sharing Movement, 2000).

25. Accordingly, the government provided 4.649 billion won out of the total 18.461 billion won in the North-South Cooperation Fund to EBCF, the Korean Welfare Foundation, ICF, WVK, Good Neighbors, KSM, and Korea JTS. This was designed to help the North Korean people in a substantial way by providing funds to secure transparency of distribution for the aid projects. Interview by the author with a Ministry of Unification official, January 2002.

26. Ministry of Unification, Notification of Revised Regulations on the Humanitarian Aid Projects for North Korea, http://www.unikorea.go.kr/kor/data/south.

27. Doug Struck, "Reverend Sun Myung Moon Makes Inroads in North Korea," *The Washington Post,* 10 November 2000.

28. Ministry of Unification, "Contact Points between the North and South Korean Civilian Organizations in Humanitarian Assistance," Memorandum of Understanding Report for the National Assembly, 2001; Chung Oknim, "ROK's Sunshine Policy and Its Support for Domestic NGOs" (in Korean), (Seoul: Sejong Research Paper 2002), p.10.

29. Chung Oknim, "The Sunshine Policy: An Interim Assessment," *Korea and World Affairs,* 24, no. 1 (spring 2000): 22.

30. Interview by the author with an NGO official, June 2001.

31. Giorgio Maragliano, "Six Years of Aid to the DPRK: A Balance and a Possible Way Forward," paper presented at the Fourth International Symposium on Korea and the Search for Peace in Northeast Asia, Kyoto, Japan, 17–19 November 2001.

32. For example, in the second inter-Korean ministerial meeting, North Korea asked for food aid, saying that it was suffering a severe food crisis due to the decline in crop yield. In response to this request, the South Korean authorities stated in a joint press release that "based on the principle of helping each other, [South Korea] would examine and pursue the possible provision of food aid in the form of loans for North Korea" (Ministry of Unification, Reports about the Second Inter-Korean Ministerial Meeting, *Tongil Sokbo,* 2000-8). In addition, in 2000 alone, the government provided 300,000 tons of fertilizer (worth $80 million or 96 billion won) to North Korea.

33. President Kim Dae Jung, "Berlin Declaration on the Inter-Korean Reconciliation and Cooperation," *Chosun Ilbo* (Seoul), 3 September 2000.

34. President Kim Dae Jung, "Berlin Declaration on the Inter-Korean Reconciliation and Cooperation," *Chosun Ilbo* (Seoul), 3 September 2000.

35. Following the inter-Korean summit talks, the government provided the following aid in 2000: 300,000 tons of fertilizer (worth 94.4 billion won or $78.63 million); 600,000 tons of food (500,000 tons in loans and 100,000 tons through the WFP); 1.5 million pieces of winter underwear for children (4.6 billion won); and purchase and logistical costs for the provision of apples, pears, and potatoes (18.1 billion won). As a result, South Korea's assistance to North Korea during 2000 amounted to $113.76 million, out of which $78.63 million was contributed by the government.

36. Lee Jong-moo, interview by the author, January 2001.

37. Korea Methodist Church Seobu Annual Conference, International Corn Foundation, North-South Sharing Campaign for Peace and Unification, National Coalition of NGOs for Inter-Korean Agricultural Development and Cooperation, Okkedongmu (Friends

Standing Shoulder to Shoulder), Children in Korea, Presbyterian Church of Korea, International Foundation for Northeast Asia Education Culture, Good People, National Council of Saemaul Undoong Movement in Korea, Medical Aid for Children of the D.P.R.Korea, Korean Sharing Movement, Won Buddhism Kangnam Temple, World Vision, Korean Committee for UNICEF, Eugene Bell Foundation, Good Friends: Center for Peace, Human Rights, and Refugees, Korea Reconciliation Committee: Roman Catholic Archdiocese of Seoul, Forest for Peace, Korea Association of Health, Korea Food for the Hungry International, Christian Council of Korea, Good Neighbors, Join Together Society, and Korea Welfare Foundation.

38. Interview with relief workers of civilian organizations engaged in helping North Korea. Materials for the Third International NGO Conference on Humanitarian Assistance to North Korea: Cooperative Efforts Beyond Food Aid, Yongin, South Korea, 17–20 June 2001, January 2001.

39. Interview by the author with officials from the Humanitarian Affairs Bureau of the Ministry of Unification, January 2002.

40. For this, the government faced criticism for providing funds only for large, existing projects while neglecting start-up projects and new organizations.

41. Interview by the author with an NGO worker, October 2001.

42. Interview by the author with Ministry of Unification officials, January 2002.

43. Kim Kyung-won and Chung Oknim, "South Korea's Engagement Policy toward North Korea: Outcomes, Problems, and Tasks" (in Korean), in *Report for the Sixth South Korea—The United States 21st Century Committee* (Seoul: World Economy Research Institute, 2000), p. 36.

44. Of course, not all civilian organizations share a common viewpoint; however, they support an engagement policy with North Korea, particularly civilian exchanges and humanitarian aid.

45. Interview by the author with NGO workers, June 2001.

46. Giorgio Maragliano, "Six Years of Aid," note 31.

47. Regarding the cause of the North Korean food crisis, see Kim Young-hoon et al., Policy Options to Promote Inter-Korean Agricultural Cooperation (in Korean), (Seoul: Korean Rural Economic Institute, 1999), pp. 24–29.

48. Ven Pomnyun, "Present Conditions and Future Questions."

49. Ministry of Unification, "Developments in the Assistance to North Korea from South Korea and other Countries in the First Half of 2001." http://www.unikorea.go.kr/kor/policy. Meanwhile, fertilizers were transported to Nampo, Songrim, Haeju, Wonsan, Heungnam, and Chungjin.

50. President Oh Jae-shik, interview, Korea World Vision, October 2001.

51. Robert Marquand, "Food Crisis Goes from Bad to Worse in North Korea: A Decade after Loss of Soviet Support, Frail Economy and Bad Weather Bring Shortages," *The Christian Science Monitor,* 17 April 2001.

52. Lee Jong-moo, "Current Status of Agricultural Cooperation."

53. Ibid.

54. Kim Un-geun, interview by Korea Rural Economic Institute (KREI), January 2002.

55. Lee Jong-moo, "Humanitarian Assistance," note 52; Kim Sun-kwon, "Current Status and Tasks."

56. Lee Jong-moo, interview by the author, June 2001.

57. Kim Sun-kwon, "Current Status and Tasks"; ICF, "The Hope of the 21st Century Flourishes in the Corn Fields, 2001," http://www.icf.or.kr; Lee Jong-moo, interview by the author, January 2002.

58. *World Vision Activity Report 2000* (in Korean), Join Together Society, October 2000.

59. North Korea was WVK's largest aid recipient in 1995.

60. Interview by the author with WVK officials, October 2001.

61. Lee Jong-moo, "Current Status of Agricultural Cooperation."

62. Interview by the author with Lee Jong-moo, June 2001.

63. Interview by the author with an NGO worker, September 2001.

64. For more information on South Korean NGOs' medical relief aid, see Park Chong-cheul, "Korean NGO Medical Relief Work for North Korea," paper presented at the Third International NGO Conference on Humanitarian Assistance to North Korea: Cooperative Efforts Beyond Food Aid, Yongin, South Korea, 17–20 June 2001, pp. 51–66; Lee Jong-moo, "Current Status of Assistance to North Korea in the Health Care and Medical Sector" (in Korean), in *Korean Sharing Movement: Materials Commemorating the Fourth Anniversary of the KSM Inauguration* (Seoul: Korean Sharing Movement, 2001), pp. 80–83.

65. Interview by the author with relief workers, June 2001.

66. Park Chong-cheul, "Korean NGO Medical Relief Work," note 64.

67. International aid sharply decreased from $358.71 million in 1999 to $106.66 million in 2000. The UN organizations responsible for health care and medical aid include the World Health Organization (WHO), UNICEF, and the UN Fund for Population Activities (UNFPA). Yet aid from these organizations totaled only $3.03 million—2.9 percent of total donations of $152.7 million.

68. Park Chong-cheul, "Korean Medical Relief Work," p. 55.

69. The North Korean medical system is based on the idea of equality, providing free medical treatment, with designated doctors for each district. Pyongyang also stresses the integration of preventive medicine into the system. Park Chong-cheul, "Korean NGO Medical Relief Work," note 64.

70. Stephen Linton, "Working with North Korea's Medical System," paper presented at the Third International NGO Conference on Humanitarian Assistance to North Korea: Cooperative Efforts Beyond Food Aid, Yongin, South Korea, 17–20 June 2001.

71. Stephen Linton, Mansfield Center for Pacific Affairs NGO Symposium on North Korea, July 2002.

72. The two had different priorities: the North had asked the foundation to build a hospital, while KWF suggested providing medical equipment. See Lee Jong-moo, "Current Status of Assistance."

73. Interview by the author with KWF officials, June, 2001.

74. Remarks by Park Chong-cheul. In September 1997, Medical Aid for Children of the D.P.R.Korea provided medicine for children's hospitals worth $300,000, revitalizing health care and medical aid to North Korea.

75. Interview by the author with a Korean Welfare Foundation worker, June 2001.

76. UNICEF report, 12 July 2001.

77. Interview by the author with a WVK official, October 2001.

78. Stephen Linton has visited North Korea many times since 1995 and maintains amicable relations with the North Korean Ministry of Foreign Affairs.

79. Written interviews by the author with NGO relief workers assigned to projects in North Korea, September 2001.

80. The APPC handles relatively large organizations such as the Korean Welfare Foundation and KSM.

81. Interview by the author with NGO workers, June 2001; Giorgio Maragliano, "Six Years of Aid," note 31.

82. Interview by the author with NGO workers, January 2001.

83. Interview by the author with NGO workers, June 2001.

84. Lee Jong-moo, "Current Status of Assistance," pp. 69–79.

85. For example, in March 2000 the EU cancelled a planned 20,000 tons of food aid to North Korea through the WFP and European NGOs and decided to send it to Kenya. Interview by the author with an NGO worker, January 2002.

Chapter Five
Lessons of the NGO Experience
in North Korea

Scott Snyder

The learning curve for nongovernmental organizations (NGOs) working inside North Korea since 1995 has been steep, and the lessons have been stark. Because of the nature of the North Korean system, in which political control has been maintained despite dramatic system failure, North Korea has provided a working environment and set of challenges unlike any other the international humanitarian relief community has faced. The North Korean leadership has made adjustments only begrudgingly. Moreover, many of the major system changes that have been made within North Korea have been outside the closely guarded view of humanitarian workers themselves, who have often been prevented from interacting with the sectors of North Korean society most desperately in need of assistance. International aid workers and NGO representatives have achieved unprecedented access to North Korea, but under strictly controlled conditions that have either concealed the most insidious aspects of the regime's struggle to maintain absolute political control or required unwitting or conscious acquiescence to them. Many workers have been ill equipped by their previous training, experience, and/or knowledge of the North Korean environment to understand and interpret what has been hidden from them, because the cracks in the system have been precisely what they have not been supposed to see. Likewise, the North Korean authorities have faced a desperate situation but have not been prepared to take the perceived political risks of allowing direct access between international aid workers and ordinary North Korean people.

Thus, it has been very difficult for humanitarian aid workers, even through monitoring activities that have come to include extensive field visits outside of Pyongyang, to get a true picture of the situation on the ground. They have been blocked from obtaining the random sampling necessary to conduct empirical studies that might determine the true severity of North Korea's food shortage. Humanitarian aid workers cannot even be sure that the impressions they have gained through direct observation of the situation have been accurate, because of the strict controls under which they have operated.

As described in the other chapters in this volume, the experience of humanitarian aid workers on the ground in North Korea has engendered widely varied responses among those NGOs involved in providing assistance to the country. Regardless of whether the initial motivation has been primarily humanitarian, intrinsically political, or a combination of the two, the result of the experience of working with North Korea has been to polarize the NGO response and catalyze external public advocacy against North Korea's political controls, opaque operating environment, and inequitable distribution of goods within its own system.

On the one hand, the severity of the working conditions, the lack of "humanitarian space" in which to operate, and the inability to judge objectively whether their work is truly providing humanitarian benefit or simply propping up a morally bankrupt regime have led some groups to pull out of North Korea. On the other hand, those who continue their work in North Korea today recognize that the situation is desperate but that the North Korean government has neither the capacity nor perhaps the political will to meet those urgent needs. Despite unsatisfactory conditions, these NGOs continue their work in hopes that their presence and continued advocacy will result in improved conditions for monitoring and will eventually stimulate internal change by providing North Korean authorities with opportunities to gain direct experience working with the international community. Anecdotal evidence suggests that, indeed, some improvements have been achieved. These success stories emphasize changes in attitude among North Korean counterparts, who have begun to understand the benefits of increased interaction with the outside world but who face enormous internal difficulties advocating for such interaction because of entrenched political interests in the North Korean system.

Some people who have visited North Korea as humanitarian aid workers have confirmed North Korea's worst suspicions about the purposes and intentions of NGO "monitoring" activities. Those individuals have gathered information embarrassing to the regime and have sent it to the outside world, resulting in publicity that has engendered suspicion and friction among North Korean watchers and has internally justified the need to keep an eye on "foreign spies" believed to have come to gather information that might be used against North Korea. For a regime that uses control of information as a vehicle for maintaining political and psychological control of its people within clearly defined boundaries, the leakage of information about North Korea's internal conditions is a significant threat. Reporting by NGO staff residents in Pyongyang to the international media about conditions inside North Korea has drawn strong responses and ultimately has led to expulsion or nonrenewal of visas for those individuals. One well-known case involved the December 2000 expulsion of a German humanitarian relief doctor, Norbert Vollertsen, after he gave a guided tour of Pyongyang to many of the visiting media delegation that had accompanied then-U.S. Secretary of State Madeleine Albright on her visit to Pyongyang in October of that year. Since that time, unencumbered by the constraints felt by those who continue their work in North Korea, Vollertsen has actively focused the media spotlight on the inequities of the North Korean system and the country's failure to treat all of its citizens in accord with minimum human rights standards.

Given the past isolation of the Democratic People's Republic of Korea (DPRK) and its policy of managing foreign influence as a way of trying to protect its system, DPRK efforts to limit international access to its population should have been quite predictable. However, by imposing strict controls on international aid workers in ways that have often prevented humanitarian NGOs from fulfilling their missions in North Korea, the North Korean authorities have succeeded in stimulating an international response that has further eroded prospects for North Korea to achieve its fundamental goal of regime survival. This has been due to the DPRK's inordinate concern with protecting its population from external influences. The North Korean leadership's tactical response of "covering up"—i.e., heightening internal political indoctrination and imposing strict internal political controls on interactions with international aid workers—while simultaneously "reaching out" to accept international assistance from an increasing number of sources has only created an international situation in which the North Korean regime is increasingly embattled and the internal status quo is increasingly unsustainable.

Far from safeguarding North Korea's regime survival, the end result of such strict political controls has been to hasten "donor fatigue" as a result of frustrations experienced on the ground in the country. Donor fatigue has decreased the amount of assistance available to North Korea through international organizations, while simultaneously catalyzing external advocacy groups on human rights and other issues, which are raising the political bar the North Korean leadership must clear to gain political acceptance in the international community and safeguard the regime's survival. Put simply, North Korea's efforts to accept international aid while maintaining political control of its population by limiting direct contacts of international aid workers with ordinary North Koreans are fundamentally incompatible and are likely to hasten the demise of the system in its current form.

NORTH KOREA'S STRATEGY TO "CONTAIN" THE SIDE EFFECTS OF INTERNATIONAL ASSISTANCE

The primary goal of the North Korean watchers assigned to be with humanitarian aid workers throughout their daily activities was to protect the pillars of the regime's strict political control in three critical areas: control of information, control of individual movement, and control of the means of production. In each of these areas, the humanitarian aid workers were regarded as the "flies and mosquitoes" of reform that the North Korean leadership most feared. One of the North Korean guides' most important jobs was to severely curtail direct personal contact between aid workers and the people of North Korea. North Korean guides became the filters and buffers through which contact was managed, particularly in light of the fact that the vast majority of international aid workers had no Korean language skills (as was North Korea's stated preference for in-country aid workers) and were thus dependent on their minders for almost everything while in North Korea.

North Korean authorities achieved their objective of control of information by adhering to the system of monitoring and guiding foreigners in their interactions with the North Korean system and limiting, to the extent possible, the available points of unmediated contact. This strategy was applied even more strictly to South Korean counterparts, who had even less access for monitoring purposes than international humanitarian aid workers. Likewise, North Korean laws prohibiting direct contact with foreigners also served as a powerful incentive for ordinary people to avoid the risks of unsupervised interaction with foreign aid workers—until the food situation became so desperate that the Public Distribution System (PDS) failed. North Korean restrictions on random access and unsupervised monitoring of food delivery points were designed to maintain control over what outsiders might know and understand of society in North Korea. Direct substantive contact with ordinary North Koreans was rare and virtually impossible outside the presence of North Korean guides. Even when humanitarian workers did have the opportunity to see direct evidence of system failure in specific sectors, the regime's obsessive control over information and the environment in which the NGOs were working prevented full disclosure of the situation in North Korea and led to many distortions in the outside world's understanding of the true conditions in the country. This was not only because humanitarian aid workers were so closely guarded that they did not have many opportunities to see the most compromising situations or interpret the significance of their observations. Many international aid workers with the greatest commitment to providing assistance were least likely to offer testimony to the outside world regarding what they saw, because they worried that their relief assistance would be lost to victims of the famine, with no guarantee that public disclosure would result in positive change inside North Korea and the possibility that the government would respond by cutting off access to populations in need.

Over time, the international humanitarian effort challenged DPRK authorities' attempts to control information in a variety of ways. The first challenge came in the form of requests to allow a sufficient number of monitors to enter North Korea to effectively conduct monitoring activities. These requests were consistently among the most contentious points between international and nongovernmental organizations and North Korean authorities. Today, six years after aid groups first entered North Korea, clear limits remain on the number of permanent representatives from these groups that the government allows in North Korea. It has become clear that one reason for these limits has been the lack of qualified personnel to guide and accompany foreign visitors. During this period, it has also become clear that there have not been enough qualified North Korean Flood Damage Rehabilitation Committee (FDRC) representatives to be assigned to all the monitoring activities of the international aid workers, which has tested the limits of the North Korean surveillance system. Mistakes and failures in coordination have provided occasional opportunities for monitors to have random or direct monitoring experiences in the course of going about their duties. Likewise, as the watchers have become familiar with the monitoring routines, occasionally they have let down their guard or acceded to individual requests for random access or individual household interviews without advance notice or preparation. One internal constraint on North Korea's willingness to allow greater numbers of monitors into the country has been the lack of trained personnel in the FDRC or related government institutions with the English language or other skills necessary to guide and surveil NGO representatives who visit North Korea. As greater amounts of aid have come into North Korea and greater numbers of guides have been required to take care of foreign visitors, the system of guidance has begun to reach the breaking point, and certain forms of random access have become possible every time a coordination detail has slipped past an overworked North Korean guide.

North Korean guides from the FDRC or the Committee for Overseas Compatriots have also controlled information flows by trying to control access to institutional end users outside of Pyongyang. Representatives from Pyongyang and local political officials have monitored contact with every regional institution in the countryside. Watchers have often suggested that the local reaction to external assistance might have been misunderstood or that those institutions might have had a negative attitude toward foreigners. However, the local institutional end users have generally been the most enthusiastic and appreciative of external assistance. One strategy employed by some NGOs has been to make promises to these aid recipients directly and publicly (in the presence of their institutional hosts and watchers)—in so doing, they are providing a measure of transparency and accountability that might have been absent in mediated communication through the central government authorities. This strategy has ensured that the local institutional head would continue to badger officials regarding the promised assistance and has decreased the possibility of diversion.

The UN World Food Program (WFP) has repeatedly tried to increase the number of food monitors in the country in order to effectively cover the geographic distribution of its deliveries. UN requests to conduct a random nutritional survey of North Korean children have been repeatedly denied. The single UN survey conducted with government cooperation in 1998 could not be called random; however, the results revealed severe rates of malnutrition among the sample population. North Korean authorities were particularly incensed that this information was publicly released and have since refused to cooperate with UN efforts to do follow-up nutritional surveys, although a new survey did take place during 2002. The U.S. Agency for International Development (USAID) has made such a survey a precondition for continuing to provide assistance through the WFP. Although international organization representatives on the ground claim to have obtained demographic data from the DPRK government that might be used to develop a more detailed understanding of conditions across the country, data of this sort are typically not shared publicly for fear of further alienating North Korean authorities. The need for basic empirical information that might be used to shed light on conditions inside North Korea, and the ongoing struggle to obtain it through methods such as a random nutritional survey, provide an excellent example of the DPRK leadership's obsessive focus on control of information as a core principle in its strategy for maintaining political control and managing its dealings with the international community. It is impossible to imagine that North Korean authorities can enjoy sustained support and benefits from the international community without increased transparency, yet demands for such transparency directly challenge the government's perception that control of information is a critical pillar in perpetuating political control.

A second core objective of the North Korean authorities in managing their current situation and limiting the possible influence of international aid workers is the control of individual movement. The best evidence of this concern lies with the North Korean authorities' consistent application of rules for humanitarian monitoring visits, which still require one-week advance notice to the authorities. Almost one-quarter of the country remains closed to monitoring activities by international organizations.

Restrictions on travel are even harsher for North Koreans themselves. The infrastructure to support travel in North Korea is particularly poor, and until the famine caused a breakdown in travel restrictions, the authorities had maintained highly restrictive policies on travel outside a citizen's region. During the harshest period of the famine, many urban residents traveled to the countryside in search of food from relatives working on farms, and internal refugees were common. The authorities were not in a position to keep starving people from taking every measure in their search for food, and the flow of refugees and representatives of particular work units in an effort to barter raw materials and stock inside the country for food was uncontrolled. At that time, travelers to the countryside reported North Koreans crammed into and on top of trains as they moved internally in search of food. Despite improved food conditions in recent years, the regime is no longer able to completely prevent internal travel or travel across the North Korea–China border completely, which increases the flow of outside information into the country. Observers who have traveled outside Pyongyang now report that individual travelers may offer packs of cigarettes and, recently, even cash to passing cars in order to hitch a ride, a practice that was unheard of before the famine. Although internal checkpoints prevent unauthorized individuals from entering Pyongyang or crossing into and out of other key districts around the country, the level of surveillance is reported to have relaxed considerably in recent years, and bribes have partially replaced official permission from the government as an effective way of gaining authorization to travel inside the country.

Humanitarian workers inside North Korea have been a part of increased travel to and from the countryside, through both inputs of resources and monitoring requirements. One unintended effect of the entry of humanitarian aid workers has been a more precise and balanced understanding of the situation inside North

Korea by elite members of the FDRC and certain other branches of the government who have traveled with international humanitarian aid workers. These individuals have the latitude and trust of the regime as well as the necessary skills to communicate with visiting humanitarian aid workers, and they can see for themselves the true situation inside their country. Some of them have grasped for the first time the nature of the problems being faced and the North Korean system's limitations. Although this group comprises a relatively small number of trusted technocrats and functionaries whose primary task has been watching the foreign humanitarian aid workers, seeing the conditions in the North Korean countryside and the gap between North Korea and the outside world must have been a jarring and eye-opening experience for them. Also, some guides have inevitably been influenced by their direct experience of the acute system needs facing North Korea. Their experience has given them a better understanding of the types of resources that certain aid organizations have been able to bring. These watchers and technocrats, who have had practical experience with outsiders and who have some measure of understanding of the outside world, are the persons most likely to be able to shepherd real change inside North Korea, if the leadership structure and environment ever give them a chance to do so.

The third objective of the DPRK regime's strategy to maintain political control is to control the means of distribution, an area that has also faced severe challenges in the context of North Korea's famine. The most obvious vehicle by which North Korean leaders have sought to achieve this objective has been the maintenance of the PDS as the primary vehicle through which outside assistance to North Korea must pass. International aid agencies such as the WFP have been required by their counterparts in North Korea to give assistance via the PDS, through which the government directs distribution of resources to various individuals and locations throughout the country. On its face, the PDS appears to be egalitarian, because the rationing system attempts to guarantee a certain amount of support to everyone eligible to receive PDS rations. However, every individual in North Korea does not appear to have access to food distributed through the PDS, and the priority of distribution is managed according to the central government's dictates and preferences. For example, as North Korea's food crisis grew increasingly severe, residents of remotely located counties or provinces, especially in the northeastern part of North Korea, were deprived of PDS rations, while people in other regions and institutions critical to the regime's survival remained privileged recipients of government aid.

Upon their arrival in North Korea, some humanitarian aid agencies were very impressed by the PDS as a vehicle through which to reach a broad sector of the North Korean population in a relatively efficient way. From the vantage point of past experience in countries where political breakdown led to the breakdown of the distribution infrastructure, the continued existence of such a distribution infrastructure must have seemed like a great advantage in the face of a severe humanitarian crisis. The WFP's first task was simply to restore through its contributions the minimum distributions of the PDS at a level necessary to sustain the North Korean population.

At the same time that the WFP was discovering the PDS in 1996, the urgency of the crisis and the PDS's failure caused the North Korean central government to invoke "self-reliance" as the principle by which individual counties, cooperatives, and work units would became responsible for their own survival through whatever means necessary. Invoking this principle drastically decreased both the central government's responsibility to provide food through the PDS and local administrative units' dependence on the central government. The urgency and severity of the crisis caused the central government to temporarily curtail or abandon for local units the principle of control over the means of production, using the resources it was able to collect internally from various work units solely to sustain party members and the military via distribution mechanisms separate from the PDS.

Local work units had no choice but to fend for themselves. In many cases, this meant gathering whatever they could find to sell—including timber and scrap metal from factories that were no longer operational—and transporting these materials to the China–North Korea border to trade for grain. This barter trade across the Chinese border became the only alternative for survival and was accompanied by barter at an individual level, despite official constitutional prohibitions on private exchange (which were removed from the constitution in a 1998 revision). Testimony from refugees shows that the crisis catalyzed a major switch in 1996–97 from reliance on the PDS as a primary source of food to reliance on the farmers markets. The spread of private farmers markets as an alternative to the PDS was inevitable and necessary as a response to the PDS failure. This alternative is now well established and is maintained through supply lines from the Chinese side of the border, as demonstrated by the types and prices of goods now available through these markets. Although farmers markets did not enjoy official sanction or encouragement by the central government through early 2002, their existence was tolerated. Today these markets have been indirectly accepted by the DPRK leadership as the primary medium of exchange across North Korea. This acceptance was shown by the central government's decision to support price, currency, and wage adjustments in Pyongyang in the summer of 2002, and is a tacit admission that the PDS can no longer function as the primary medium of exchange in North Korea.

The devolution of control over the means of production to the county, cooperative, and work-unit levels was clearly a temporary measure at a time when the central government had no alternatives. Through at least 1999, hope remained within some quarters of the leadership that the central government would eventually be able to restore its distribution monopoly and reassert its unchallenged political control. However, the establishment of local markets, the increased availability of foreign currency through barter and trade, and the dependence on those markets for daily necessities have made the PDS—especially outside Pyongyang—a secondary, relatively undependable vehicle for obtaining food.

This devolution has eased the severity of the situation for recipients who may not have developed good access to hard currency or who do not have goods to barter for food in local markets. The amount of food distributed through the PDS is no longer an accurate indicator of imminent distress within the North Korean system, yet it has remained the WFP's primary indicator of distress and the primary vehicle through which the WFP distributes food inside the country. In this respect, the WFP is an ally of the government in its efforts to reestablish control over the means of production. The channeling of all humanitarian food assistance through the PDS to institutions officially designated by the DPRK government has been the primary strategy employed in the North Korean leadership's attempt to maintain control over the distribution of external assistance in ways that support rather than threaten the regime's stability. The announcement in the summer of 2002 of adjustments in prices, wages, and currency exchange rates in Pyongyang is direct evidence of the need for the WFP to abandon the PDS and find a new, more market-oriented vehicle for distribution of humanitarian assistance.

THE NGO EXPERIENCE IN NORTH KOREA: LESSONS AND NEXT STEPS

Despite the many frustrations and difficulties in precisely measuring the effectiveness of the humanitarian response to North Korea's food crisis, its impact on internal change in the country, or the value of the experience in terms of understanding reality inside North Korea, a number of lessons can be drawn from the NGO experience in the DPRK that may be valuable in assessing future NGO efforts and determining the most effective means of interacting with North Korea in the future.

First, NGOs have been, and continue to be, an expanded source of knowledge about conditions inside North Korea, despite North Korean efforts to block such understanding by inhibiting direct contact with average North Korean people. Before 1996, there were very few opportunities to gather direct information about conditions inside North Korea or to have contact with North Korean institutions other than via the small diplomatic community, which itself is cloistered and isolated. And even those diplomatic representatives were subject to the same types of controls that have now been extended to NGOs and UN organizations with resident representation in North Korea. However, NGO experience in North Korea cannot be effectively evaluated without combining information gained on the ground with testimony from refugees. The testimony of refugees and defectors—much of which is being collected and documented by South Korean NGOs conducting humanitarian operations along the border between China and North Korea and in South Korea—is essential to an understanding of the conditions inside North Korea and the North Korean leadership's motivations in maintaining such tight controls on NGO humanitarian and development activities in the country. Both perspectives are needed because they show the extent and limits of the government's efforts to maintain control and/or tolerate reforms internally.

Second, the NGO presence—whether intentionally or accidentally—presents a direct challenge to the North Korean regime's capacity to manage information, movement, and the means of production. For this reason, great efforts have been made by the DPRK government to control and box in NGO representatives, even by imposing limitations that inhibit NGO abilities to provide effective humanitarian assistance. Although NGO representatives operate in a constrained environment inside North Korea, their presence itself requires the time and resources of North Korean authorities, and this on occasion has tested the ability of the North Korean government to maintain strict limits on NGO monitoring activities. Thus far, North Korean control mechanisms have largely been effective in keeping NGO and UN monitors inside a box, although occasional cracks in the system have occurred because of manpower limitations on the North Korean side or sheer perseverance on the part of committed individuals with extensive experience working in Korea. In addition, some have noted that the North Korean authorities make different efforts to provide insights during assessment missions than they do during routine monitoring activities, that high-ranking officials are given better access than normal food monitors, and that nonresident organizations are provided with preferential access in comparison with the level of access possible for resident NGO representatives. Likewise, North Korean representatives assigned as watchers to NGO monitors or other visitors are exposed to a broader than usual range of experiences and messages that strengthen their understanding of the situation in their country. In some cases, the insights the watchers have gained have helped them become internal advocates of the type of assistance that would be more useful to North Korea's well-being in the long run, rather than focusing strictly on the conditions necessary to achieve the political objective of regime survival. Any expanded assistance must be accompanied by appropriate capacity on the part of NGOs and UN organizations to complete without undue interference the tasks they are assigned while in North Korea.

Third, the greatest value of NGO efforts in North Korea lies in setting new precedents and expanding access and opportunities for interaction between North Korea and the outside world. In general, NGO efforts appear to have been more effective in this regard than international organization or UN efforts, which through their reliance on the PDS system deliver assistance to North Korea while accepting at face value DPRK decisions about the end users of that assistance. To the extent possible, NGOs should focus on projects that allow them to develop grassroots counterparts outside Pyongyang at the county or local level, rather than relying on the government to provide the interface between central and local levels. The greater the contact with and penetration of the project to the grassroots of North Korean society, the more likely it is that the project will be effective in achieving its core objectives. Often, projects that reach outside Pyongyang also provide coordination benefits to the DPRK government in terms of facilitating contacts that might otherwise not be possible between local- and central-level counterparts.

Fourth, North Korean attempts to control NGO representatives at the expense of their ability to do their jobs will inevitably create more external pressure on the regime. Resentful of the situation they face or the obstacles placed on their activities by the DPRK government, disaffected NGOs will lobby for conditions that make it more difficult for the North Korean regime to survive. The result will be that in the absence of evidence that the DPRK government is prepared to undertake major system reforms, there will be growing pressure from foreign governments and international organizations. There will also be increased skepticism about the long-term viability of the North Korean regime and the prospects for working together to provide the North Korean leadership with the external resources it needs to ensure its survival. By its handling of its hesitant opening to the international community while attempting to limit the internal impact of humanitarian NGOs on North Korean society, the DPRK leadership has put itself deeper into a vise, rather than taking the steps necessary to ensure its long-term viability and survival. The more deeply disaffected the NGO community becomes as a result of constraints imposed on its ability to do good through its work, the stronger the momentum for NGO-led external public criticism of North Korea will become. Foreign governments will respond by minimizing the very assistance without which the North Korean regime can no longer survive.

This dilemma is best illustrated by the transition to a new stage in the relief efforts in North Korea as the humanitarian situation has stabilized; namely, development rather than humanitarian assistance as the major focus of external programs in North Korea. As has been illustrated in earlier chapters, North Korea has accepted food assistance while resisting minimum monitoring requirements. But development assistance requires an investment in capacity-building, education, and training programs that necessitates greatly expanded North Korean contact with the outside world for longer periods of time. This contact extends beyond the political level to technical specialists and is made more difficult, if not impossible, by the insertion of political watchers designed to mediate such contacts. Although through its joint work on the Agricultural Recovery and Environmental Protection (AREP) plan, the UN has tried to introduce technical assistance projects to identify capacity-building projects in the agricultural sphere, that effort has been inhibited by the tendency of North Korean officials to look at the AREP effort as an opportunity to raise a budget from external sources to meet their own hardware and infrastructure needs without entertaining serious reforms. The European Union has offered a substantial program of exchange and training for North Korean experts on a range of critical issues, including institutional support and capacity-building, technical assistance in the energy field, rural development and reforestation, and enhancing North Korea's transportation infrastructure. Considerably more attention and commitment will be necessary to draw out North Korean technical experts who can be effectively trained to expand the government's capacity to meet the needs of its people using a variety of new methods. However, such a program will require the DPRK leadership's sustained commitment to allow North Korean specialist participation in long-term programs outside the country and increased exposure by large numbers of specialists to large-scale training programs operating inside North Korea. Whether the North Korean leadership can move forward to train large numbers of technical experts abroad and then allow them to apply their learning to create the system changes necessary to support North Korea's vast economic development needs will be the litmus test that will shape the next phase of NGO interaction with North Korea.

The North Korean leadership's response will determine whether the North Korean system will remake itself by its own efforts or be overwhelmed by a chain of events beyond its control. More than good intentions from the NGO sector, counterpart governments, or the DPRK leadership will be necessary to manage the next phase of involvement in North Korea, given a leadership that, according to the principle of *juche*, continues to pave its own wide, clear road to the future.

Appendices

Appendix A:
International Community Aid to the DPRK (1995-2001)

Period	Target (USD)	Result (USD)	Note ($1,000) *
9/95–6/96	20,320,000	9,270,000	U.S. – 2,225; Japan – 500; EU – 380 (46%)
7/96–3/97	43,640,000	34,700,000	U.S. – 7,170; Japan – 6,000; S. Korea – 3,390; EU – 8,600 (80%)
4/97–12/97	184,390,000	157,810,000	U.S. – 45,370; Japan – 27,000; S. Korea – 26,330; EU – 27,520 (84%)
1/98–12/98	383,240,000	215,870,000	U.S. – 171,850; EU – 13,800; S. Korea – 11,000; Canada – 3,950; Norway – 2,390; Egypt – 2,800; Australia – 1,320; Czech. Repub. – 20 (56%)
1/99–12/99	393,440,000	226,300,000	U.S. – 175,000; EU – 7,980; Sweden – 3,830; Canada – 3,400; Australia –2,700; Norway – 2,000; Denmark – 1,950; Finland – 720; Ireland – 270 (52%)
1/00–12/00	331,710,000	106,660,000	UN – 90,670; Individual countries – 2,600; Int'l NGOs – 15,730
1/01–12/01		258,490,000	UN – 213,890; Individual countries – 17,530; Int'l NGOs – 27,070

Total Aid (1995–2001): $1,009,100,000

Source: ROK Ministry of Unification

(www.unikorea.go.kr/kor/policy/human_view.php?db=Tab_2&boardno=925&content=C34/C3429.htm&code=230&flag=1)

* Not all countries represented

Appendix B:
South Korean Government Aid to the DPRK (1995-2001)

Year	Aid Amount (USD)	Note
1995	232,000,000	Rice – 150,000 tons
1996	3,050,000	WFP – $2,000,000 (mixed grain) UNICEF – $1,000,000 (powdered milk 203 tons) WHO – $50,000
1997	26,670,000	WFP – $6 million (mixed grains 9,852 tons) UNICEF – $340,000 (ORS factory cost) WFP – $10,530,000 (corn 50,000 tons; powdered milk 300 tons) UN – $9.8 million WFP – $4 million (CSB 8,389 tons) UNICEF – $3.6 million (powdered milk 781 tons) WHO – $700,000 UNDP – $1.2 million FAO – $300,000
1998	11,000,000	WFP – $11,000,000 (corn 30,000 tons; flour 10,000 tons)
1999	28,250,000	Fertilizer – 1.15 million tons Total: 33.9 billion won
2000	78,630,000	Fertilizer – 500,000 tons Additional fertilizer aid – 100,000 tons
2001	70,450,000	Underwear – 1.5 million articles Fertilizer – 200,000 tons WFP – corn 100,000 tons WHO – medicine for malaria

Total Aid (1995–2001): $450,050,000

Source: ROK Ministry of Unification

Appendix C:
South Korean NGO Aid to the DPRK (1995-2001)

Period	Aid Amount	Note
9/95–5/97 through IFRC	4,960,000	Flour (3,664 tons), powdered milk (94 tons), blankets (10,000), vegetable oil (1.86 million tons), ramen (100,000 packages), socks (305,000 pairs), potatoes (1,900 tons), radish seeds (4.8 tons), cabbage seeds (6.4 tons), corn (4,980 tons)
6/97–7/97 Korean RC – 1st shipment	8,500,000	Corn (41,511 tons), flour (2,000 tons), ramen (150,000 boxes), fertilizer (2,000 tons), (corn, standard 53,841 tons)
8/97–10/97 Korean RC – 2nd shipment	8,900,000	Corn (17,100 tons), sorghum (14,576 tons), flour (5,501 tons), vegetable oil (270,000 tons), potatoes (1,300 tons), baby food (96.74 tons), powdered milk (100 tons), children's vitamins (30,000 bottles)
3/98	170,000	Fertilizer (800 tons)
4/98–6/98 Korean RC – 3rd shipment	9,350,000	Corn (16,585 tons), flour (13,500 tons), vegetable oil, powdered milk, fertilizer, salt, rice, potatoes, socks, Korean cows, and others
9/98–12/98 additional aid	11,330,000	Jung Ju-yung: corn, cows NGOs: corn, flour, white rice, powdered milk, sugar, vegetable oil, etc.
1/99–12/99	18,630,000	Korean Red Cross: fertilizer (3/30-6/5), (40,000 tons) Through Korean Red Cross: 3.4 trillion won from 24 organizations: flour (3,139 tons), corn (4,015 tons), powdered milk (42 tons), sugar (165 tons), seed potatoes (180 tons), vegetable oil (15,845 liters), ramen (9,930 boxes), clothing (215,448 articles), medical supplies, etc. Independent channel (bilateral): 6.6 trillion won from 10 organizations: EBCF: medical equipment worth 1.2 trillion won South-North Sharing Campaign: clothing, flour, fertilizer, sprayers, shovels, etc., worth 1.1 trillion won Good Neighbors: pasteurizing tanks, cream separators, veterinary medicine, etc., worth 33 million won JTS: fertilizer (384 tons), dental equipment, sugar (52 tons), powdered milk (30 tons), notebooks, pencils, etc., worth 356 million won

Continued on page 128

Appendix C:
South Korean NGO Aid to the DPRK (1995-2001)
Continued

Period	Aid Amount	Note
1/99–12/99	18,630,000	WVK: medicine, greenhouse material, seed potatoes (1.5 tons), clothing (24,871 articles), etc., worth 390 million won KSM: clothing (46,500 articles), fabric, medicine, corn (1,000 tons), flour (51 tons), ramen (300 boxes), eggs (5 million), tangerines (585 tons), goats (450), etc., worth 2.6 trillion won Korean Rotary Foundation: ambulance, medicine, etc., worth 40 million won ICF: 10 types of seed potatoes, worth 1 million won Nat'l Episcopal Committee for the Reconciliation of Korean People: fertilizer (1,000 tons), corn (3,000 tons), clothing (5,500 articles), shoes (1,000 pairs), etc., worth 791 million won National Reconciliation Buddhist Committee: shoes (5,000 pairs), clothing (6,828 articles), etc., worth 207 million won
1/00–12/00	35,130,000	Korean Red Cross: ≈$94,416 (16 organizations)
		Independent Channel: ≈$256,166 (13 organizations)
1/01–12/01	64,940,000	Korean Red Cross: ≈$238,333
		Independent Channel: ≈$465,000 (19 organizations)

Total Aid (1995–2001): $161,910,000

Source: ROK Ministry of Unification

Appendix D:
Food Assessment for the DPRK (1996-2002)
Cereal Supply/Demand (000 tons)

Year	1996/ 1997	1997/ 1998	1998/ 1999	1999/ 2000	2000/ 2001	2001/ 2002
Total Availability	**2,995**	**2,663**	**3,481**	**3,472**	**2,920**	**3,656**
Production	2,837	2,663	3,481	3,472	2,920	3,656
Stock Draw-down	158	0	0	0	0	0
Total Utilization	**5,359**	**4,614**	**4,835**	**4,765**	**4,785**	**4,957**
Food Use	3,798	3,874	3,925	3,814	3,871	3,855
Feed Use	600	300	300	300	300	300
Other Uses (seed, losses, industrial)	645	440	610	651	614	802
Closing Stocks	316	0	0	0	0	0
Need/Import Requirement	**2,364**	**1,951**	**1,354**	**1,293**	**1,865**	**1,301**
Commercial Imports	500	700	300	300	700	100
Pledged Food Assistance	30	241	360	370	600	819
Uncovered Import Requirement	1,834	1,010	1,054	623	1,165	382

Source: UN World Food Program

Appendix E:
DPRK Cereal Production (1995/96–2001/02)

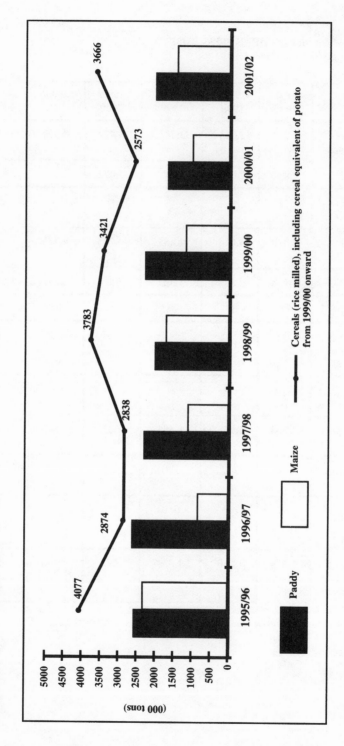

Source: UN World Food Program

Appendix F:
DPRK Estimated Cereal Import Requirements (1995/96–2001/02)

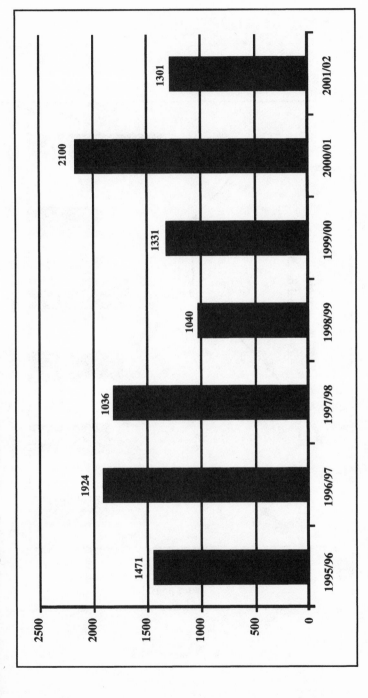

Source: UN World Food Program

Appendix G:
DPRK Food Aid Compared with the Total Estimated Cereal Deficit (1995–2001)

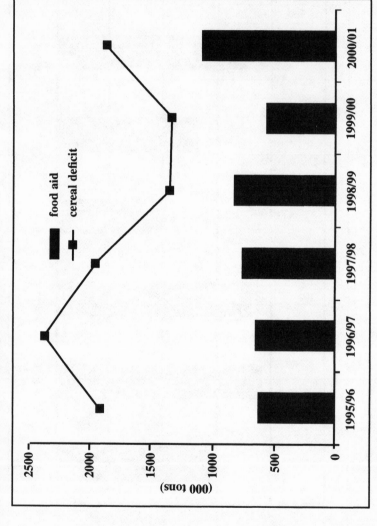

Source: UN World Food Program

Appendix H:
Value of NGO Food Aid to the DPRK (1996–2001)

REPUBLIC OF KOREA						
NGO	**AMOUNT BY YEAR**					
	1996	**1997**	**1998**	**1999**	**2000**	**2001**
EBCF	814	4,620	0	0	0	0
FKI	0	11,183	6,000	0	0	0
GNK	0	1,240	60	0	600	1,125
Hyundai	0	0	70,000	0	0	0
JTS	0	396	396	396	411	396
KBOA	0	0	0	0	0	18
KCF	0	0	150	0	0	1,000
KJCM	0	0	0	0	0	4,000
KMA	0	0	0	0	105.4	0
KNAC	0	0	0	0	0	12,000
KRC	0	51,885	99,392	0	20	0
KRCC	0	0	0	0	2,700	3,200
KSM	0	0	0	0	6,256	2,617
KUC	0	0	0	0	0	150
KWF	0	0	0	0	20	17
LIONS	0	0	0	0	240	0
Nestle Corp.	0	0	29	0	0	0
OKBM	0	0	0	0	160	329
OKDM	0	0	0	0	510	0
WVK	100	3,600	3,600	3,600	3,600	3,600
Total	**914**	**72,924**	**179,627**	**3,996**	**14,622.4**	**28,452**

Continued on page 134

Appendix H:
Value of NGO Food Aid to the DPRK (1996–2001)
Continued

	EUROPE					
NGO	**AMOUNT BY YEAR**					
	1996	**1997**	**1998**	**1999**	**2000**	**2001**
ACT	2,030	3,970	5,000	2,000	0	0
ADRA	38	272	118	0	0	0
CAD	0	192	0	0	0	0
CAMM	100	0	0	0	0	0
Caritas (HK)	10,006	29,164	25,000	10,000	21,291	2,107
CfC	100	0	360	0	0	0
CESVI	0	0	23	0	0	0
CWW	0	0	495	0	0	0
GAA	0	0	11,795	0	0	0
HBAid	0	0	45	0	0	0
IFRC	45,255	72,841	10,000	0	0	0
Cap Anamur	0	0	5,000	0	0	0
MSF	0	0	20	0	0	0
Oxfam	320	0	0	0	0	0
PMU Interlife	145	1,000	15,000	0	0	0
Taize Comm	0	0	878	0	0	0
Total	**57,994**	**107,439**	**73,734**	**12,000**	**21,291**	**2,107**

Continued on page 135

Appendix H:
Value of NGO Food Aid to the DPRK (1996–2001)
Continued

UNITED STATES						
NGO	**AMOUNT BY YEAR**					
	1996	**1997**	**1998**	**1999**	**2000**	**2001**
ADM	0	0	327	0	0	0
CHSM	0	0	0	0	36	35
CWS	0	1,676	113	0	0	61
FHI	0	255	0	0	0	0
FTC	180	0	0	0	0	0
KAP	0	0	360	0	0	0
KASM	0	5,211	0	0	0	0
LDSC	80	0	180	0	1,000	0
MCI	50	19	0	0	0	0
SBAP	160	0	0	0	0	0
UMCOR	0	300	0	0	0	0
WSC	0	868	0	0	0	0
WVI	1,640	1,040	301	0	0	0
Total	**2,110**	**9,369**	**1,281**	**0**	**1,036**	**96**

Source: UN World Food Program; unit: metric ton

Appendix I:
NGO Food Aid to the DPRK by Region (1996–2001)

Region	1996	1997	1998	1999	2000	2001	Total
ROK	914	72,924	179,627	3,996	14,622	28,452	300,535
Europe	57,994	107,439	60,234	12,000	21,291	2,107	261,065
United States	2,110	8,501	1,281	0	1,036	96	13,024

Source: UN World Food Program; unit: metric ton

Chronology

1995

August

The Democratic People's Republic of Korea (DPRK) requests that the UN Department of Humanitarian Affairs (UNDHA) appeal for emergency assistance. A UN Disaster Assessment and Coordination (UNDAC) team and World Health Organization (WHO) representative arrive in Pyongyang.

September

The first consignment of relief supplies is officially handed over to North Korea and distributed to flood-affected areas near Sinuiju, North Pyongan province.

November

The International Federation of Red Cross and Red Crescent Societies (IFRC) completes its first distribution of quilts, blankets, and clothing to 20,003 families in North Pyongan, North and South Hwanghae, Chagang, and Kangwon provinces.

Médecins Sans Frontières (MSF) begins a program to maintain mortality from main diseases at an acceptable level and to deter and prevent outbreaks of epidemics and malnutrition.

1996

January

South Korean religious groups organize a Peace Conference to plead for assistance for North Korean flood victims.

February

The U.S. Agency for International Development (USAID) announces that it will provide $2 million to the UN World Food Program's (WFP) emergency appeal for the growing food crisis in North Korea caused by severe floods.

March

Civilian organizations in South Korea launch a campaign to help North Koreans suffering from devastation by floods.

April

The United Methodist Committee on Relief (UMCOR) receives a U.S. Department of Commerce license to ship $100,000 worth of humanitarian supplies to North Korea.

June

USAID provides $6.2 million of Public Law 480 (Title II) humanitarian assistance.

At the DPRK's invitation, the Carter Center, with support from the Rockefeller Foundation, sends a team of agricultural experts to North Korea.

The Korean Sharing Movement (KSM) is launched to assist North Koreans and pursue national reconciliation. It collects donations from public campaigns and attracts public attention to the need to provide assistance to the Northern brethren. KSM provides 50,000 bags of flour to North Korea, a project in which 33 people, representing six religious orders along with civilian organizations, are involved.

July

One hundred thousand tons of food arrive in North Korea from the Chinese Communist Party and the Chinese government.

December

The Humanitarian Affairs Bureau is formed within the South Korean Ministry of Unification. The new bureau will take full responsibility for humanitarian aid to North Korea.

1997

Several European NGOs achieve residency status in the DPRK: Campus for Christus (CfC, Switzerland), Children's Aid Direct (CAD, UK), Concern Worldwide (CWW, Ireland), Cooperazione e Sviluppo (CESVI, Italy), Médecins du Monde (MDM, France), Médecins Sans Frontières (MSF, French, Dutch, and Belgian sections), and German Agro Action (GAA, Germany).

February

South Korea plans to donate $6 million in emergency food aid to famine-threatened North Korea, despite recent tensions over a high-ranking North Korean defector who sought asylum at the South Korean Embassy in Beijing.

March

International organizations and Koreans living in Yanbian and Manchuria reveal that North Korea's food distribution system has collapsed.

KSM invites staff members from the Eugene Bell Centennial Foundation (EBCF) and the World Council of Churches (WCC) to hold an international congress on the food crisis in North Korea.

The Korean American Sharing Movement (KASM), representing Korean American interests, appeals for $5 million worth of humanitarian aid for starving North Koreans.

May

South and North Korean Red Cross organizations reach an agreement on direct delivery of aid.

June

A South Korean ship sets sail for North Korea, carrying the first direct sea shipment of South Korean Red Cross food aid since the North initially appealed for international help in 1995.

Japan expresses a willingness to join President Bill Clinton in providing more aid to famine-stricken North Korea. Japanese prime minister Hashimoto Ryutaro hints he is prepared to drop his refusal to give aid to North Korea.

August

Human Rights Committee chairperson Christine Chanet expresses deep concern over the DPRK's announced intention to withdraw from the International Covenant on Civil and Political Rights.

September

In response to a UN appeal to the world community, the Japanese government and ruling Liberal Democratic Party officials state that Japan is set to grant North Korea 70,000 tons of food aid. Japan would offer the aid package through the United Nations as humanitarian assistance, although Pyongyang is calling for bilateral aid from the country.

November

The joint Federation-DPRK Red Cross relief operation shifts its main focus from food aid (begun in September 1995) to improving the quality and quantity of health care.

1998

January

The European Commission (EC) approves an additional package of humanitarian aid worth ECU 10 million for North Koreans suffering the consequences of a severe humanitarian crisis.

More than 1 million individual packets of vegetable seeds arrive in Pyongyang on January 3, 1998, from the Adventist Development and Relief Agency International (ADRA) Canada office.

February

The U.S. State Department announces that the United States will donate 200,000 metric tons of food aid to North Korea.

Reports from China say that thousands of North Koreans are crossing the Chinese border to escape the famine, which has claimed at least 2 million lives. The *South China Morning Post* says that many of the refugees, who have crossed the frozen Yalu River into China, are begging for food and shelter in small border towns and villages.

A North Korean diplomat who defected to South Korea earlier this month says that the North's economic crisis is worsening and people's discontent is boiling to the surface. "North Korea's current economic hardship is at its worst and its agriculture is in a shambles," says Kim Dong-soo, 38, who was a diplomat based in Rome.

March

Red Cross officials from North and South Korea open talks in Beijing to discuss food aid desperately needed by Pyongyang as North Korea's grain stocks dry up.

April

Australia gives North Korea emergency aid worth $2 million to buy 8,000 tons of cereals and to pay for health services, medicines, and vaccines provided by UNICEF.

North Korea is accused of moving too slowly in allowing UN monitoring of food aid distribution. WFP executive director Catherine Bertini says that Pyongyang had still not allowed UN agency monitors to visit 49 of the country's 210 counties. She says the WFP would not deliver aid to areas where it could not monitor distribution.

May

In the face of continuing food shortages in North Korea, the EC launches an integrated package of food aid and support for agricultural rehabilitation worth ECU 30 million.

North Korean authorities give the WFP permission to distribute and monitor food aid in 171 of the 210 counties to which the UN food relief agency has requested access.

June

A visiting Vatican delegation to North Korea makes a "substantial contribution" on behalf of Pope John Paul II.

July

MDM decides to withdraw from North Korea, citing severe constraints to liberty of movement and consequent inability to monitor effectively.

August

Famine in North Korea has killed 300,000 to 800,000 people a year in the past three years, a U.S. congressional team says after visiting the country. Members of the U.S. House of Representatives International Relations Committee say this figure derives from reports by the UN, NGOs, and refugees.

UNICEF says that the incidence of malnourished children appears to be declining in certain parts of North Korea. In a press statement, UNICEF says that the situation has improved in accessible areas. According to the United Nations agency, its staff have reported seeing declining numbers of malnourished children during field visits this year.

September

North Korea agrees to a U.S. request that it resume Four-Party Talks (United States, China, North and South Korea) in October.

The United States contributes an additional 300,000 metric tons of wheat to the WFP's DPRK program.

MSF pulls out of North Korea in protest against the way in which aid was being distributed. In public criticism of the North Korean government, MSF says that the Stalinist state faces widespread famine, but adds that aid is being handed out in a discriminatory fashion and the authorities are preventing outsiders from making an independent assessment of the situation.

For the first time, the South Korean government allows some civilian organizations to supply North Korea with relief goods directly, letting these NGOs share this role with the South Korean National Red Cross, which had monopolized the aid channel to the North.

October

A senior WFP official says that he is confident that international aid has not been diverted away from famine-stricken North Korean citizens and is reaching the needy.

South Korea approves the Hyundai business group's plan to dispatch a herd of cattle to famine-stricken North Korea, according to a government spokesman:

"The government approved Hyundai's plan to send the cattle to the North after Pyongyang said its misunderstanding over the death of cattle that had been sent earlier was resolved."

A former South Korean prisoner of war, who recently escaped from famine-stricken North Korea, says that a growing number of people there are trying to sell their blood to smugglers to survive, according to Seoul's Defense Ministry.

November

Representative Tony Hall (D-OH) says that North Korea faces a critical shortage of food and medicine, along with an increase in infectious diseases. He says Washington should "do whatever [it] need[s] to do to get medicines in there," including easing the 48-year U.S. embargo on North Korea.

Aid agencies in North Korea establish the "Common Humanitarian Action Plan" in response to the withdrawal of several medical relief organizations; most prominently, MDM and MSF. The plan outlines a set of fundamental principles for implementing aid: assessment, monitoring, and evaluation.

1999

January

Red Cross officials in South Korea send food and clothing to help ease famine in North Korea, according to South Korean officials. The aid includes 2,000 tons of flour, 1,700 boxes of biscuits for children, and clothing.

February

The South Korean government officially adopts a multiple-channel policy, opening more channels for contacts with North Korea and allowing civilian organizations to help North Korea independently.

March

South Korea sends 5,000 tons of fertilizer aid to North Korea following the DPRK's agreement to allow U.S. inspections of a suspected nuclear site.

April

Japan says that North Korea must make constructive concessions on its missile program and other issues before Japan can resume food aid to the country.

May

The International Corn Foundation (ICF) says that it will send 2,000 tons of fertilizer, 100 bicycles, and 40,000 tassel bags to North Korea.

The United States announces that it will provide an additional 400,000 tons of food aid to North Korea, amid signs that a major diplomatic push to ease tensions on the Korean Peninsula is in the works.

June

Amnesty International (AI) says in its annual review that the North Korean people remain vulnerable to hidden human rights violations, since the Stalinist country cannot be adequately monitored. Restrictions on access and information hamper the collection of independent and impartial information about the human rights situation in the reclusive state.

December

Japanese foreign minister Kono Yohei rules out immediate food aid to North Korea, despite the two countries' agreement to hold more talks on establishing diplomatic ties. During two-day talks in Beijing, Tokyo and Pyongyang agreed to meet again in an effort to resume talks on the establishment of diplomatic relations.

The Oxford Committee for Famine Relief (Oxfam), one of the biggest and oldest humanitarian NGOs, decides to withdraw from North Korea. Oxfam was implementing a European Community Humanitarian Office (ECHO)-funded water treatment program in Pyongyang, South Pyongan, and North and South Hwanghae. Like other organizations, Oxfam cited poor accountability and lack of demonstrable impact as the reasons for its withdrawal.

2000

January

Japanese prime minister Obuchi Keizo says that he will work toward normalizing his country's diplomatic ties with North Korea. Japan, unnerved by North Korea's launch of the Taepodong missile in August 1998 over Japanese territory, hopes engagement with the Pyongyang regime can help defuse the threat of future launches.

February

Famine-hit North Korea admits it had been ravaged by its worst-ever energy shortage, blaming the debacle on natural disasters and a U.S. stranglehold on its nuclear industry.

March

Japan endorses a 3.84 billion yen ($36.6 million) grant to the WFP to provide 100,000 tons of rice to North Korea.

Haaretz newspaper says that Israel is ready to join a U.S.-led initiative to aid North Korea if it freezes its nuclear weapons program and arms deliveries to the Middle East. Israel is the only country in Europe and Asia to have responded favorably to a U.S. request to take part in an international assistance scheme for Pyongyang.

Action Contre La Faim (ACF), a French-based aid organization specializing in nutrition, food security, health, and water treatment, pulls out of North Korea. Limited accessibility, distorted representation of beneficiaries, and rejection of a request for authorization to establish street kitchens are the main reasons for the organization's withdrawal.

The Cooperative for Assistance and Relief Everywhere, Inc. (CARE) withdraws from North Korea for the reason that the operational environment in the country has not progressed to a point where the organization feels it is possible to implement effective rehabilitation programs—in spite of its four-year efforts with the North Korean government to improve access, transparency, and accountability.

April

South Korean President Kim Dae Jung pledges hefty financial aid to cash-strapped North Korea—including credit loans—for agreeing to an inter-Korean summit. Analysts see Kim's comment leading to a string of ambitious inter-Korean projects after the June 12–14 summit to rebuild the North's tattered economy.

Chinese police authorities confirm that North Korean refugees, facing repatriation to their famine-hit homeland, had rioted at an internment camp in northeastern China and had taken a number of guards hostage.

June

DPRK leader Kim Jong Il and ROK President Kim Dae Jung meet in Pyongyang.

The United States eases economic sanctions against North Korea after almost 50 years, further lowering the barriers between the reclusive Stalinist state and the international community. The move implements an announcement made by President Bill Clinton in September 1999. It is aimed at improving relations between the two nations, while encouraging North Korea to refrain from testing long-range missiles.

David Morton, the UN Development Program's (UNDP) North Korea representative, says that in the future, famine-stricken North Korea will receive help in reviving its industrial sector, as well as food and agricultural aid. Interest in broadening aid to cover the industrial sector is expressed during a meeting of 21 donor countries and senior North Korean officials in Geneva.

July

South Korea pledges a new shipment of fertilizer to famine-hit North Korea as a means of speeding up inter-Korean reconciliation.

August

Japan's Foreign Ministry says that it will send a mission to North Korea to see if its rice aid for the famine-hit Stalinist state has been properly distributed.

A delegation from the South Korean conglomerate Hyundai crosses into North Korea through the truce village of Panmunjom with a symbolic gift of 500 cattle to ease the Stalinist state's food crisis. Led by Chung Mong-hun, son of ailing Hyundai founder Chung Ju-yung and head of the conglomerate's North Korean ventures, the delegation is expected to discuss Hyundai's business projects during two days of talks.

September

South Korea's Ministry of Unification announces that it will offer 500,000 tons of food aid to North Korea as a long-term loan. On top of the food aid loan, the South will donate another 100,000 tons of corn to the WFP for the North.

November

Representative Tony Hall (D-Ohio) says that the North Korean famine has grown worse in the past year, with children and the sick suffering especially. In a November 29 news release, Mr. Hall urges countries concerned with conditions in North Korea to "renew international efforts to fight a famine that has worsened in the past year." The Pyongyang regime's 21 million people are suffering not only from a lack of food, but also from a lack of medicine and fuel to counter the bitter cold of Korea's winter, he said.

December

The EC approves 600,000 euros in emergency humanitarian aid for North Korea. The aid, channelled though ECHO, will finance winter clothing for 36,000 children of kindergarten age (4–7 years) in the mountainous North Pyongan province. Some 9,000 blankets are also being supplied for distribution to flood victims.

2001

January

Norbert Vollertsen, a German doctor who was thrown out of North Korea, says that the people of the isolated Stalinist state are suffering "burnout syndrome," with widespread alcoholism adding to crippling food and power shortages.

February

An EU economic team visits North Korea to study the state's energy and agriculture problems and assess what help can be given.

March

International Monetary Fund (IMF) president Horst Koehler proposes a joint survey with South Korea and the World Bank to help rebuild the North's tattered economy.

China pledges a free shipment of 15,000 tons of diesel oil to North Korea to help ease energy and food shortages in the impoverished communist country.

April

German foreign cooperation and development minister Heidmarier Wieczorek-Zeul announces the German government's pledge of 30,000 tons of surplus beef to North Korea.

Vietnam donates 5,000 tons of rice and other humanitarian aid to North Korea.

Swedish officials say that the EU will press Pyongyang on human rights and economic reform when a top-level EU delegation travels to North and South Korea to promote the peace process.

May

Visiting EU leaders state that North Korean leader Kim Jong Il has agreed to an unprecedented human rights dialogue with the EU. After five hours of talks, EU external affairs commissioner Chris Patten claims a breakthrough with the reclusive Stalinist leader in tackling North Korea's appalling human rights record.

The U.S. government decides to provide 100,000 tons of food aid to North Korea following a request from the WFP. The delivery will be the first such aid to North Korea by the administration of President George W. Bush.

New Zealand's prime minister Helen Clark says that her country will donate $84,000 to UNICEF's programs in North Korea.

June

President Bush announces on June 6 his decision to undertake "serious discussions" with North Korea on issues such as North Korea's nuclear activities and missile programs.

Experts say North Korea, grappling with chronic food shortages, has been parched by its worst spring drought in more than 80 years and needs more international aid to feed its people.

Seven North Koreans arrive in Seoul—four days after they sought help at the Beijing office of the UN High Commissioner for Refugees (UNHCR), requesting to go to South Korea. After the concurrence of South Korea was obtained, Chinese authorities, in an arrangement with UNHCR, agreed to the departure of the North Koreans on humanitarian grounds.

July

The White House says in a memo that President Bush has authorized the release of $20 million to purchase heavy fuel for North Korea, in compliance with a 1994 Agreed Framework.

November

South Korean unification minister Hong Soon-young says that Seoul will not give large-scale food aid to North Korea unless Pyongyang carries out agreed-upon reunions of separated families. Hong makes the statement as the two Koreas are set to resume high-level talks in the North's Mt. Kumgang.

A shipment of 6,000 tons of German beef arrives in North Korea.

WHO director-general Gro Harlem Brundtland warns that more money is needed to prevent a major health crisis in North Korea. On a visit to North Korea, she states that the reemergence of malaria after a 20-year absence will likely affect 300,000 people by the end of the year. She launches an appeal for $8 million to support "development and emergency efforts" in North Korea.

The WFP urges the international community to support a new $214 million emergency operation in the DPRK aiming to feed 6.4 million people in 2002. Despite the increase in domestic food production in 2001, it is not enough to provide the country's population with the minimum requirement. At least 611,000 metric tons of cereals and commodities are required.

December

The United States announces a plan to provide 105,000 tons of food commodities to be administered by the U.S. Department of Agriculture's (USDA) Foreign Agricultural Service in response to the WFP's request for continued donations to support emergency feeding operations in North Korea. The amount to be donated breaks down into the following: 49,910 tons of wheat; 20,090 tons of soybeans; 15,000 tons of vegetable oil; 15,000 tons of rice; and 5,000 tons of nonfat dry milk.

South Korea announces plans to donate 100,000 tons of food to North Korea. Unification minister Hong Soon-young states that 100,000 metric tons of corn will be donated to the North via the WFP. He also says that the South would be ready to discuss donating an additional 300,000 tons of rice to the North, should Pyongyang return to the negotiating table.

Eighteen North Korean refugees defect to South Korea, including three families. Despite the easing of the economic difficulties and food shortage this year, more North Koreans have fled their homes in recent years. Compared with the 312 who defected last year, there are 570 defectors this year.

2002

January

North Korea admits to an increasing energy shortage that makes it difficult to ensure heating; an adequate supply of drinking water; and lighting in public buildings, apartment buildings, and other residential quarters. This is attributed to the U.S. administration's failure to deliver on the U.S.-DPRK Agreed Framework, in which the United States promised to provide two light-water reactors, each with a capacity of 1 million kw by 2003 in return for the DPRK's pledge to freeze construction on its nuclear power facilities and to operate them only for peaceful purposes.

March

The first food aid shipment of the year, bearing 23,500 tons of corn, arrives in North Korea. This is the first batch of 100,000 promised this year.

It is estimated that food aid to North Korea could run out by summer, due to the major shortfall in international donations caused by the international focus on the plight of Afghanistan. According to the WFP, only 155,000 tons of the requested 611,200 of aid (25 percent) are secured, with the United States donating 55,000 tons and the rest coming from South Korea.

A group of 25 North Koreans seeks asylum at the Spanish Embassy in Beijing and requests to be sent to South Korea. They appeal to be recognized as refugees.

The EC decides to provide 5.55 million euros to the DPRK. The money is to be allocated through ECHO and targets just under 250,000 people. This aid is to repair and construct water and sewerage systems, and to increase the capacity of clean water distribution networks serving local populations and rural communities in five of the country's provinces.

Japan will not give food aid unless progress is made in the alleged kidnapping of Japanese nationals by the communist state. However, Japan's prime minister Koizumi Junichiro states that a door will be open for dialogue with Pyongyang.

AI expresses concern that the Chinese government's recent announcement of a renewed crackdown on "illegal immigrants" is aimed at North Koreans.

The Institute for Strategic Reconciliation, an independent think tank based in the United States, decides to send medical supplies worth $1.65 million to help about 260,000 children, pregnant women, and disabled people. It will be distributed to hospitals in North Hamgyong province, Hamhung province, Kangwon province, Shinuiju city, etc.

April

The South Korean government decides to provide North Korea with 200,000 tons of fertilizer after considering the country's earlier request for fertilizer assistance during the visit of South Korea's special envoy, Lim Dong-won. The first batch is to be sent this month and the delivery is expected to be complete by the end of May. The cost is expected to be $54 million (66 billion won) and to come from the Inter-Korean Cooperation Fund. The decision is also made to disburse $630,000 (780 million won) from the Inter-Korean Cooperation Fund for the fourth round of reunions of separated families. The exchange is to take place April 28 at Mt. Kumgang.

China announces that it will provide $6 million in material aid to North Korea to commemorate what would have been the 90th birthday of the late North Korean leader Kim Il Sung.

The undersecretary-general for humanitarian affairs and emergency relief coordination states that more than 6 million people in North Korea will face life-threatening shortages of food, basic medicines, and clean drinking water unless donor countries act quickly. More than $230 million is needed—80 percent of the $258 million requested for the DPRK. Only $23.5 million has been collected, which is only 10 percent of the amount required.

May

The United Nations Global Fund will extend about $5 million in aid to North Korea for treating three major diseases: AIDS, tuberculosis, and malaria.

Relief organization Handicap International (HI) announces that it may have to pull out of North Korea due to lack of resources.

Germany announces that it will send a third shipment of beef to North Korea.

Some 250 South Korean food donors visit North Korea days after the latest breakdown of inter-Korean talks. The citizens of Jeju, a southern island of South Korea, are invited to visit by the North in appreciation for donating tangerines over the past four years.

A Christian humanitarian organization in Canada announces its decision to send 7,000 tons of wheat to North Korea to help fight famine.

A North Korean defector and former high-ranking intelligence officer of North Korea's National Security Defense, Yun Seong-su, pushes for an end to international aid to the country, saying that it does not reach the vulnerable and is used for the military. He believes that the international community should help North Koreans flee the country and grant them international refugee status.

June

The last portion of the 200,000-ton fertilizer aid promised to the DPRK is sent. Urea and compound fertilizer in the amount of 6,000 tons is sent to North Korea.

The DPRK recognizes the IFRC as a legitimate relief organization and grants it legal status in the DPRK. This allows the organization to conduct relief activities legally on a permanent basis and expand its operations. It may be possible for the IFRC to work in the off-limit areas. It is estimated that about 20 to 25 percent of the population still has no access to aid.

USAID announces that it will provide an additional 100,000 tons of food aid to the DPRK, fulfilling the baseline donation.

The WFP announces that 150,000 tons of additional food aid is needed to prevent severe shortages later in the year.

The Australian government announces that it will provide $6 million in humanitarian aid to the DPRK through the WFP. This will allow approximately 11,400 tons of wheat to be bought from Australian farmers and shipped out to North Korea.

It is reported that North Koreans are resorting to eating grass and seaweed to fight off hunger, as UN food aid has been cut off due to lack of donations. The WFP is forced to suspend food deliveries to school children and the elderly in dire need of assistance, due to the lack of donations.

Vietnam announces that it will provide the DPRK with 5,000 tons of rice worth $1 million to help North Korea fight its food shortage.

A naval clash occurs between South and North Korean warships in the Yellow Sea, killing four South Korean sailors and leaving many injured.

July

The South Korean government announces that it will withhold its aid packages to the DPRK, including the previously arranged 30 metric tons of rice, in the aftermath of the naval clash. Kim Dae Jung issues a strong warning to the North and expresses his intention to retaliate should the North attempt another military attack.

Acronyms

ACF: Action Contre La Faim

ACT: Action by Churches Together

ADM: Archer Daniels Midland

ADRA: Adventist Development and Relief Agency International

AFSC: American Friends Service Committee

AI: Amnesty International

APPC: Asia Pacific Peace Committee

AREP: Agricultural Recovery and Environmental Protection

CAD: Children's Aid Direct

CAMM: Christian Association for Medical Mission

CARE: Cooperative for Assistance and Relief Everywhere, Inc.

Caritas International: The Catholic Agency for Overseas Aid and Development

CESVI: Cooperazione e Sviluppo

CfC: Campus for Christus, Switzerland

CFGB: Canadian Foodgrains Bank

CHSM: Children's Home Society of Minnesota

CRS: Catholic Relief Services

CWS: Church World Service

CWW: Concern Worldwide

DMZ: Demilitarized Zone

DOTS: Directly Observed Treatment System

DPRK: Democratic People's Republic of Korea

EBCF: Eugene Bell Centennial Foundation

EC: European Commission

EC DG/DEV: European Commission's Directorate-General for Development

ECHO: European Commission's Humanitarian Aid Office

FALU: UN Food Aid Liaison Unit

FAO: UN Food and Agriculture Organization

FDRC: Flood Damage Rehabilitation Committee

FFW: Food for Work

FHI: Food for the Hungry International

FKI: Federation of Korean Industries

FTC: Feed the Children

GAA: German Agro Action

GAO: U.S. General Accounting Office

GNK: Good Neighbors Korea

HBAid: Hungarian Baptist Aid

HI: Handicap International

IAEA: International Atomic Energy Agency

ICF: International Corn Foundation

IFRC: International Federation of Red Cross and Red Crescent Societies

IMF: International Monetary Fund

JTS: Join Together Society

KAP: Korean American Presbyterians

KASM: Korean American Sharing Movement

KBOA: Korea Buddhist Order Association

KCF: Korean Christian Federation

KEDO: Korean Peninsula Energy Development Organization

KJCM: Korea Jeju Citizens Movement to Help the North

KMA: Korean Medical Association

KNAC: Korean National Agricultural Cooperative Federation

KRC: Korean Red Cross

KRCC: Korea Reconciliation Committee of Concord

KREI: Korea Rural Economic Institute

KSM: Korean Sharing Movement

KUC: Korea Ulsan City Association

KWF: Korea Welfare Foundation

LDSC: Latter-day Saints Charities

MCC: Mennonite Central Committee

MCI: Mercy Corps International

MDM: Médecins du Monde

MSF: Médecins Sans Frontières

NGO: Nongovernmental organization

NIS: National Intelligence Service

OCHA: UN Office for the Coordinator of Humanitarian Affairs

OKBM: One Korea Buddhist Movement

Oxfam: Oxford Committee for Famine Relief

Oxfam GB: Oxford Committee for Famine Relief, Great Britain

PDS: Public Distribution System

PMU InterLife: PingstMissionens Utveck-lingssamarbete (development-aid branch of the Swedish Pentecostal Mission)

PRC: People's Republic of China

PUF: Committee for the Peaceful Unification of the Fatherland

PVOC: Private Voluntary Organization Consortium

ROK: Republic of Korea

SBAP: Southern Baptist

SIDA: Swedish International Development Cooperation Agency

UMCOR: United Methodist Committee on Relief

UN: United Nations

UNDAC: UN Disaster Assessment and Coordination

UNDHA: UN Department of Humanitarian Affairs

UNDP: UN Development Program

UNFPA: UN Fund for Population Activities

UNHCR: UN High Commissioner for Refugees

UNICEF: UN Children's Fund

UNOCHA: UN Office for the Coordination of Humanitarian Affairs

USAID: U.S. Agency for International Development

USDA: U.S. Department of Agriculture

WCC: World Council of Churches

WFP: World Food Program

WHO: World Health Organization

WSC: World Summit Council

WVI: World Vision International

WVK: World Vision Korea

YMCA: Young Men's Christian Association

Further Reading

Buzo, Adrian. *Guerilla Dynasty: Politics and Leadership in North Korea.* Bou Colo.: Westview Press, 1999.

Downs, Chuck. *Over the Line: North Korea's Negotiating Strategy.* Washington, ᴅ.ᴄ.. American Enterprise Institute, 1999.

Eberstadt, Nicholas. *The End of North Korea,* Washington, D.C.: American Enterprise Institute, 1999.

Harrison, Selig S. *Korean Endgame: A Strategy for Reunification and U.S. Disengagement.* Princeton, N.J.: Princeton University Press, 2002.

Hunter, Helen-Louise and Stephen J. Hunter. *Kim Il-Sung's North Korea.* Westport, Conn.: Praeger Publishing, 1999.

Kang, Chol-Hwan and Pierre Rigoulot. *The Aquariums of Pyongyang: Ten Years in a North Korean Gulag.* Trans. Yair Reiner. New York: Basic Books, 2001.

Kim, Samuel S., Tai-Hwan Lee and Tai-Hee Lee, eds. *North Korea in Northeast Asia.* Lanham, Md. and Boulder, Colo.: Rowman and Littlefield, 2002.

Levin, Norman D. and Yong-Sup Han. *Sunshine in Korea: the South Korean Debate over Policies toward North Korea.* Washington, D.C.: RAND Corporation, 2002.

Moltz, James Clay and Alexander Mansourov, eds. *The North Korean Nuclear Program: Security, Strategy, and New Perspectives from Russia.* New York and London: Routledge, 1999.

Natsios, Andrew. *The Great North Korean Famine.* Washington, D.C.: U.S. Institute of Peace, 2000.

Noland, Marcus and C. Fred Bergsten. *Avoiding the Apocalypse: Economic Turmoil on the Korean Peninsula.* Washington, D.C.: Institute of International Economics, 2000.

Oberdorfer, Don. *The Two Koreas: A Contemporary History.* Rev. ed. Cambridge, Mass.: Perseus, 2002.

Oh, Kongdan and Ralph C. Hassig. *North Korea Through the Looking Glass.* Washington D.C.: The Brookings Institution, 2000.

Snyder, Scott. *Negotiating on the Edge: North Korean Negotiating Behavior.* Washington, D.C.: U.S. Institute of Peace, 1999.

Index

Note: Page numbers followed by letters *f, n,* and *t* refer to figures, notes, and tables, respectively.

A

Academy of Agricultural Science of North Korea, 97
access, NGO: improvements in, 62–63; random, opportunities for, 115; restrictions on, 44, 52; unprecedented, 111
ACF. *See* Action Contre La Faim
Action by Churches Together (ACT), 26; food aid by, 134*t*
Action Contre La Faim (ACF), 55; activities of, 50, 55; disappointment with program results, 57; geographical location of projects, 51–52; residency status for, 49; stand on policy toward North Korea, 73–74; withdrawal from North Korea, 7, 49, 54, 57, 143–144
Adventist Development and Relief Agency International (ADRA): agricultural assistance by, 140; food aid by, 134*t*; in Food Aid Liaison Unit, 27; in North Korea Working Group, 26; in Private Voluntary Organization Consortium, 29; projects of, 33, 34, 60; residency status for, 49; success of, 31
Africa, humanitarian operations in, 21
AFSC. *See* American Friends Service Committee

Agreed Framework. *See* Geneva Agreement
agricultural assistance: European NGOs and, 48; North Korean goals for, 48; U.S. NGOs and, 33. *See also* agricultural rehabilitation
Agricultural Recovery and Environmental Protection (AREP) plan, 9, 65, 121
agricultural rehabilitation: European NGOs and, 60–61; North Korean preference for, 67–68; South Korean NGOs and, 88, 96–98
agriculture, North Korean, 19, 66; assessment of, 69
AI. *See* Amnesty International
Albright, Madeleine, 112–113
alcoholism, in North Korea, 145
American Friends Service Committee (AFSC): in North Korea Working Group, 26; success of, 31; training and capacity building by, 35
Amigos Internacionales, 29
Amnesty International (AI), 143
Anderson, Mary B., 64
APPC. *See* Asia Pacific Peace Committee
Archer Daniels Midland (ADM), food aid provided by, 22*t,* 135*t*
AREP. *See* Agricultural Recovery and Environmental Protection plan
Asia Foundation, training by, 35
Asia Pacific Peace Committee (APPC), 9–10, 26, 102–103; and inter-Korean

Contributors

CHUNG OKNIM

Chung Oknim is a Korea Broadcasting Service commentator and an Advisory Committee member for the Ministry of Science and Technology in South Korea. Previously, she was a fellow at the Center for Northeast Asian Policy Studies, Brookings Institution (1999–2000), a visiting scholar at the Hoover Institution (1996–97), and a post-doctoral fellow at Stanford University (1995–96). She has taught at Korea University, Stanford University and Hanyang University. Dr. Chung has also served as a member of the Junior Advisory Group of the National Security Council at Chongwa-Dae and the Ministry of Unification. Her published works include a book entitled *Five Hundred and Eighty-Eight Days of the North Korean Nuclear Crisis* (in Korean, 1995) and numerous articles in both English and Korean on U.S.-Korea security relations, the Asian financial crisis, and North Korea. Dr. Chung received her B.A., M.A., and Ph.D. degrees in political science from Korea University, department of political science and international relations.

L. GORDON FLAKE

L. Gordon Flake was appointed executive director of the Mansfield Center for Pacific Affairs in February 1999. Prior to joining the Mansfield Center, Flake was a senior fellow and associate director of the Program on Conflict Resolution at The Atlantic Council of the United States. Previously, he served as director for research and academic affairs at the Korea Economic Institute of America. Mr. Flake has published extensively on policy issues in Asia, and he travels frequently to Japan, Korea, China and other countries in Asia as a conference participant and lecturer. He is a regular contributor on Korea issues in the U.S. and Asian press, and he has traveled to North Korea on four occasions. Mr. Flake was born in Rehoboth, New Mexico. Flake received a B.A. degree in Korean with a minor in international relations from Brigham Young University in Provo, Utah. He completed his M.A. at the David M. Kennedy Center for International and Area Studies, also at B.Y.U. His master's thesis was on the economic reforms in Laos. He lived in Korea for a number of years and speaks both fluent Korean and Laotian.

MICHAEL SCHLOMS

Michael Schloms is a visiting scholar at Social Science Research Center Berlin (WZB). Previously he served as assistant to a member of the German Parliament and held internships at the Ministry of European Affairs, Federal State of Brandenburg, and Doctors Without Borders (MSF), Paris. He is scholar of the Foundation of the German Economy (SDW). Mr. Schloms' publications include *Divide et Impera: Totalitärer Staat und Humanitäre Hilfe in Nordkorea* (Social Science Research Center) and "Humanitarian NGOs in Peace Processes" in *International Peacekeeping*, Vol. 10, No. 1, Spring 2003. Schloms received a German-French M.A. degree in political and social science from the Free University of Berlin/Institut d'Etudes Politiques de Paris and an M.A. degree in political science from the Free University of Berlin. As a Ph.D. candidate, his thesis topic is "The Ethics of Humanitarian Action: The Case of North Korea."

SCOTT SNYDER

Scott Snyder is the Asia Foundation's representative in Seoul, Korea, where he manages a small grant program designed to support the strengthening of Korean political and economic institution building and international relations. Previously, he was program officer in the Research and Studies Department of the U.S. Institute of Peace, where he conducted research on Asian security issues and wrote a book entitled *Negotiating on the Edge: North Korean Negotiating Behavior*. In 1998-99, Snyder conducted independent research in Tokyo and Seoul as an Abe Fellow of the Social Sciences Research Council. In addition to numerous articles on Northeast Asian security affairs with a focus on Korea, Snyder has written on the political and security implications of the Asian financial crisis and on regional island disputes in Asia, including the conflicting maritime claims in the South China Sea. Prior to joining the U.S. Institute of Peace, Snyder served as acting director of the New York-based Asia Society's Contemporary Affairs program. Snyder received a B.A. degree from Rice University and an M.A. from the Regional Studies–East Asia Program at Harvard University. He was the recipient of a Thomas G. Watson Fellowship in 1987-88 and attended Yonsei University in South Korea.